# Bobbing Head
## FIELD GUIDE

Lou Criscione

*Values and Identification*

©2005 Lou Criscione

Published by

**kp books**
*An Imprint of F+W Publications*

**700 East State Street • Iola, WI 54990-0001**
**715-445-2214 • 888-457-2873**

Our toll-free number to place an order or obtain
a free catalog is (800) 258-0929.

Library of Congress Catalog Number: 2005924814

ISBN: 0-89689-250-6

Designed by Jamie Griffin

Edited by Kristine Manty

Printed in United States of America

# Acknowledgments

I would like to express special thanks to my dear friends and fellow collectors who opened up their collections for this book. I could not have completed this project without help from Matt Boardman's amazing baseball and non-sports collection, John Pergine for his incredible AFL and NFL dolls, Joe Marasco for his diligent work with providing dolls from his spectacular hockey collection, and Dave Lebowitz for his time while I photographed his eclectic selection of dolls.

Three football bobbing head dolls displayed their own cases.

# Contents

# Contents

# Introduction

Over the last 15 years, the hobby of collecting bobbing head dolls has exploded (or should I say re-exploded) onto the scene. It has now become a mainstream collectible. What was once a 1960s novelty item sold at candy stores and sports stadiums has now become a cult collectible with an increasing number of fanatics joining in each year.

More than 20 years ago, I was reacquainted with these colorful, funny and totally addicting treasures of my youth. While at a local baseball card store, I couldn't keep my eyes off of three vintage baseball bobbing head dolls. They seemed to be nodding their approval as I reminisced about going to Yankee Stadium with my father and brother. My dad would always let us pick out a souvenir and invariably one of us would choose a bobbing head doll. After a few months of sitting on a shelf in our room, they would usually end up as target practice for our BB gun. These dolls invoke good memories. Little did I know that day, that as the storeowner wrapped up my three dolls, it would be the beginning of my passion. Since then, I have bought, sold and traded hundreds of these incredible little figures.

When I started collecting in the early 1980s, these dolls were considered a low-end item of memorabilia and I could buy almost any doll for a little more than its original 1960's cost. As the hobby grew and more collectors realized their display-ability, values skyrocketed. It is not unusual to see a doll sell for hundreds and in some cases thousands of dollars. The Internet has provided another outlet to find and sell these little reminders of our youth. With the recent trend of new stadium giveaways of bobbing head dolls, even more attention has been brought to this growing hobby.

The goal of this book is to give a brief history of these dolls, show how to care for and display them, give tips on what to look for and avoid and give a nice sampling of pictures and values. My guess is that many of you will also be smitten by the beauty of these dolls and the memories of simpler times.

## History

Most collectors agree that the "Golden Age" of the bobbing head doll was from 1960 to 1972. The majority of these dolls were made out of papier-mâché. They were, for the most part, produced in Japan for major distribution in the U.S. There were hundreds of both sport and non-sport dolls issued during this period.

During the late 1950s/early 1960s, professional sports enjoyed a major increase in popularity. This was mainly the result of increased broadcasts of sporting events on television. Baseball, and especially football, became "big business" for television networks and as a result, more fans were born. Attendance at games increased and so did the need for quality souvenirs. In 1960, the first of the sports bobbing heads were introduced at stadiums, stores and through mail order. Two separate series of Major League baseball and NFL team dolls were sold during their respective seasons. They became so popular among young fans that over the course of the next 12 years, there were seven major series of baseball dolls and more than 14 different football series. Hockey and basketball dolls were also issued during this time. As the popularity of these dolls grew, enterprising manufacturers capitalized on this craze by producing a large amount of non-sport bobbing heads that included television personalities, political figures, cartoon characters, advertising mascots and a host of humorous novelty dolls. The average purchase price of a doll ranged from $1-$2.

During the 1970s and 1980s, there was a number of bobbing head dolls issued made of plastic and ceramic composition. They never quite enjoyed the same popularity of the dolls of the 1960s, but the 1990s brought new life to the hobby. Major League teams used bobbing head give-away days at the stadium to increase attendance. Popular players of hometown teams were immortalized with their own bobbing head dolls. Several companies also started and soon there were hundreds of new bobbing heads on the scene. Fans young and old seemed to be attracted to these dolls and as they became more popular, new interest in the vintage dolls also enjoyed revitalization. There is no reason to believe that this upward trend will not continue in future years.

# Tips on Collecting and Displaying

## What dolls should I invest in?

Collecting these dolls should be a hobby and not done for monetary gain. It may be that a doll you buy will increase in value over the years, and if that happens, it is a bonus to your collecting. You should only collect these "cuties" because you like them. They should be displayed and enjoyed every day. Never buy a doll because of its potential to increase in value, but rather that it provides you with "eye candy."

As you will see in the price guide, many of the vintage dolls will not come cheaply, so if you invest with your heart and not your wallet, you will never get hurt.

## Where do I look to buy these dolls?

Collecting is a life-long avocation and as the proverb goes, "Patience is a virtue." A collector can look in antique malls, collectible shows, trade papers and flea markets with very little success, but remember: the "thrill is in the hunt." It may be that most of the time you'll get shut out at these venues, but when you do score a doll for your collection, it will be rewarding. If you are in the hobby long enough, every collector has his tale of the big find. Buying on the Internet has made collecting a little easier, but it does have its pitfalls. Pictures on the Internet may be deceiving and the seller may not be accurately describing the condition. If you do buy mail order, find a few reputable dealers that you trust and stick with them. When buying through the mail, make sure that the seller has a liberal return policy to protect your investment.

## Why have prices escalated over the last few years?

As the hobby has gained more notoriety, there are an increasing number of collectors. Since there were a limited amount of vintage dolls produced and much fewer that survived, the law of "Supply and Demand" has taken over. For hardcore collectors, once a doll has entered their collections it generally stays there. For each doll sold, there is one less on the market. Another reason for the increasing price is that most of the dolls are being offered at auction rather than through direct sale. Many times, collectors who need to "fill" in a particular doll for their collection will bid higher then they would ordinarily pay. If there are two collectors vying for the same piece, the price can be driven to beyond its suggested book value.

## How should I care for and display my dolls?

Because these dolls are so colorful and fun to look at, you'll want to display them so you can view them everyday. A secure glass case with no direct sunlight is the best for showing off your collection. A mirror back and light are great, but remember only to use the light for small time periods as it can lead to fading of color. I always suggest that the heads be stuffed with cotton balls. By pushing the cotton balls up into the head, they will not

Bobbing head dolls are so colorful
and fun to look at, they're best displayed
in a secure glass case, as this collection is.

be seen and will ultimately prevent the doll's head from bobbing into the shoulders. Unless your floors are made of concrete, most floors give a little and these dolls will be nodding back and forth. This continued action might cause damage, especially in the delicate head area. Trust me: cotton balls work and they are not obtrusive in any way.

Clean your dolls! Over the course of months and years, all dolls will build up dust and possibly grime. A simple light detergent (never anything with ammonia or harsh chemicals) and a damp cloth (not soaking wet) will make your dolls sparkle. I have also found that a light rub of Armoral will bring life back to a dull-looking doll.

If you are moving or need to ship the dolls, remember to wrap the necks with tissue paper so that there can be no movement. Even the slightest vibration can cause cracking and chipping, so take the time to wrap them carefully.

## What about restoration and repair?

This is a very "touchy" and controversial issue. It is, of course, always best to buy not only a bobbing head doll, but also any collectible, in its original condition. That being said, if a doll has problems and does not display well, what's wrong with restoring it to its original look? If you had a "classic" car from the 1960s with a smashed fender and bad paint job, wouldn't you get it repaired? Remember, however, that just like the classic car, an original condition doll is worth more than one that has been worked on—so be careful and pay accordingly.

## How can I tell if a doll has been restored or repaired?

Since many of the dolls are being "worked on" by professional artists, it is difficult even for those who handle dolls daily to detect some restoration. There are some obvious things to look for. Since the head is the main area where we find restoration, look carefully inside of it. If there is a build-up of composition, that may be an indication of repair. Many cracks are repaired on the outside of the head, but on the inside a semblance of the crack may be seen. Collectors have started to use a "black light" to try to detect new work, but unless you know what you are looking for this can be a dangerous tool. You will see different patterns on almost every doll and the novice will always jump to the conclusion that the doll has been repaired. My best advice is to, again, buy from people you trust.

## The biggest tip I can give you

Have fun! Start slow, get educated and buy dolls you like. Don't get too crazed with condition. I have seen collectors scrutinize with a magnifying glass to find imperfections that are not noticeable to the naked eye. It's really not worth the effort. A hobby is supposed to be pleasurable and stress free. Be patient and stay within your budget. If you are not comfortable with a price, don't buy it; wait for one you feel good about. The worse feeling in the world is to feel like you overpaid for an item.

## Value guide

The prices noted are the approximate value for excellent and near mint condition dolls. Because of their delicate composition, mint dolls are hard to find, and a significant premium is paid for dolls found in mint condition. On the other end of the spectrum, dolls in poor condition are not highly collectible and worth only a small fraction of the Ex/NM values. Remember, the prices given are just a guide to the dolls' rarity—prices can fluctuate greatly, especially in an auction scenario. Many of the values are based on actual prices realized in auctions and direct sale prices over the last couple of years. The rest are purely subjective, using my more than 20 years of involvement in the hobby. Use the guide as reference, but always pay prices you are comfortable with. Please buy these dolls with the intention of having fun.

If you would like to contact me, you can do so at the following:

Lou Criscione
c/o Inside the Park Collectibles
10 Churchill Drive
New Hyde Park, N.Y. 11040
516-747-7932
email: sharlou28@aol.com
Web site: www.insidetheparkcollectibles.com

# Price Guide

## Baseball Bobbing Heads

The following is a brief synopsis of the seven major series that comprise the "Golden Age" of baseball bobbing heads. During this period, there were also several oddball and rogue dolls that do not fall into any specific series. In the years that followed and up until the present time, there have been a number of other series made with different compositions ranging from ceramic to plastic.

### 1960-1961 square color base

These are generally considered the first sports series of bobbing head dolls. They are approximately 6-1/2 inches tall. There were only 12 Major League teams represented and three Pacific Coast League teams. There are no known examples of the Chicago White Sox, Cleveland Indians, Detroit Tigers, Kansas City As, Milwaukee Braves, Philadelphia Phillies and St. Louis Cardinals. The N.Y. Mets doll was actually issued before the team's inaugural season of 1962. Most of these dolls are made totally of papier-mâché, but several can also be found with wood bases. The base colors differ with each team. All have boy heads, with the exception of the Baltimore Orioles and the Pittsburgh Pirates, which have mascot heads. The "key" and rarest doll in the series is the Washington Senators. All dolls were sold in a plain cardboard box worth about $10.

| Team | Color of base | EX/NM |
|------|---------------|-------|
| Baltimore Orioles | Green (diamond shape), mascot bird head | $200/$250 |
| Boston Red Sox | Green | $250/$450 |
| Chicago Cubs | Light blue | $175/$275 |
| Cincinnati Reds | Red | $250/$500 |
| Los Angeles Angels | Dark blue | $100/$150 |
| Los Angeles Dodgers | Orange (wood) | $150/$200 |
| Minnesota Twins | Dark blue | $60/$100 |
| New York Mets | Light blue | $225/$350 |
| New York Yankees | Orange | $150/$200 |
| Pittsburgh Pirates | Gold–mascot Pirate head | $150/$200 |
| San Francisco Giants | Orange (comes with wood or papier-mâché base) | $150/$200 |
| Washington Senators | Dark blue | $1,000/$1,600 |

### Pacific Coast League

| Team | Color of base | EX/NM |
|------|---------------|-------|
| Portland Beavers | Orange | $175/$225 |
| Seattle Rainiers | Orange | $300/$450 |
| Tacoma Giants | Orange | $175/$225 |

Baltimore Orioles, mascot bird head, green (diamond shape) base, **$200-$250.**

Boston Red
Sox, green
square base,
**$250-$450.**

Chicago Cubs, light
blue square base,
**$175-$275.**

Cincinnati Reds,
red square base,
**$250-$500.**

Los Angeles
Angels, dark blue
square base,
**$100-$150.**

Los Angeles
Dodgers, orange
(wood) square base,
**$150-$200.**

Minnesota Twins, dark blue square base, **$60-$100.**

New York Mets, light
blue square base,
**$225-$350.**

New York Yankees,
orange square base,
**$150-$200.**

Pittsburgh Pirates, gold, mascot Pirate head, **$150-$200.**

Portland Beavers,
orange square base,
**$175-$225.**

San Francisco Giants, orange square base, comes with wood or papier-mâché base, **$150-$200.**

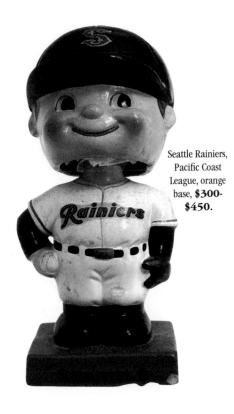

Seattle Rainiers,
Pacific Coast
League, orange
base, **$300-
$450.**

Tacoma Giants,
Pacific Coast
League, orange base,
**$175-$225.**

Washington
Senators, dark
blue square
base, **$1,000-
$1,600.**

## 1961-1963 white base

This baseball series is considered by most collectors to be the premier set. The series is comprehensive with all of the then 20 Major League teams represented. As the name indicates, all have a white base and measure 7 to 7-1/2 inches tall. Most have the boy head (several different styles), with nine of the teams having mascot heads. There are several significant variations of city names and uniform colors. The dolls can hold either a bat or ball and glove in their hands. These dolls were sold in either a picture box (pictured actual doll) or a generic box with baseball player label and team names stamped on one panel. Picture boxes can increase the value of the doll as much as $100. Generic boxes are worth about $15.

Also lumped with this series are four actual player dolls of Mickey Mantle, Roger Maris, Willie Mays and the elusive Roberto Clemente. These are the only four player dolls issued during the "Golden Age." The Mantle and Maris dolls were sold in picture boxes that alone can sell for up to $200. Mays and Clemente were sold in generic boxes with names stamped on one panel and the boxes are worth from $25 to $50.

| Team | Variations/head style | EX/NM |
|------|----------------------|-------|
| Anaheim Angels | Paper label over the base decal, rare variation of Angels doll | $200/$350 |
| Baltimore Orioles | Mascot bird head, diamond-shaped base | $300/$450 |
| Boston Red Sox | Boy head | $175/$250 |
| Chicago Cubs | Mascot bear head | $300/$450 |
| Chicago White Sox | Boy head | $200/$325 |
| Cincinnati Reds | Mascot Mr. Redlegs head | $350/$500 |
| Cleveland Indians | Mascot Indian head | $400/$600 |
| Detroit Tigers | Mascot tiger head | $225/$350 |
| Houston Colt 45s | Mascot cowboy head | $225/$350 |
| Houston Colt 45s | Mascot cowboy head with painted blue uniform, rare | $600/$1,200 |
| Los Angeles Angels | Boy head | $150/$225 |
| Los Angeles Dodgers | Boy head, either embossed lettering or decals across chest | $125/$200 |
| Kansas City Athletics | Boy head | $200/$325 |
| Milwaukee Braves | Mascot Braves head | $350/$500 |
| Minnesota Twins | Boy head | $200/$325 |
| Minneapolis Twins | Boy head, very rare variation with only three known examples | $1,000/$2,000 |
| New York Mets | Boy head, comes with dark blue or light blue uniform | $300/$425 |
| New York Yankees | Boy head | $175/$250 |
| Philadelphia Phillies | Boy head | $175/$250 |
| Pittsburgh Pirates | Mascot pirate head | $500/$750 |
| St. Louis Cardinals | Mascot bird head, diamond-shaped base | $500/$750 |
| San Francisco Giants | Boy head, either embossed lettering or decal across chest | $200/$325 |
| Washington Senators | Boy head | $250/$375 |

**Player dolls**

| | | |
|------|----------------------|-------|
| Mickey Mantle | Facsimile autograph decaled on base, square or round base | $650/$900 |
| Roger Maris | Facsimile autograph decaled on base | $450/$600 |
| Willie Mays | Facsimile autograph decaled on base, can come with dark or lighter features; there is a rarer gold base variation | $450/$600 |
| Roberto Clemente | Facsimile autograph decaled on base, rare doll | $1,500/$2,500 |

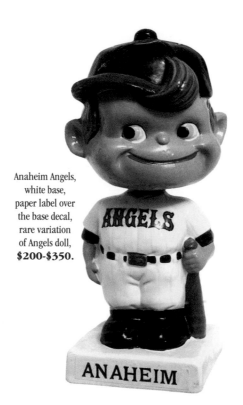

Anaheim Angels, white base, paper label over the base decal, rare variation of Angels doll, **$200-$350.**

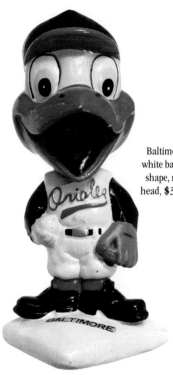

Baltimore Orioles, white base, diamond shape, mascot bird head, **$300-$450.**

Boston Red Sox,
white base, boy head,
**$175-$250.**

Chicago Cubs,
white base,
mascot bear head,
**$300-$450.**

Chicago White Sox,
mini, boy head,
**$200-$325.**

Cincinnati Reds,
white base, mascot
Mr. Redlegs head,
**$350-$500.**

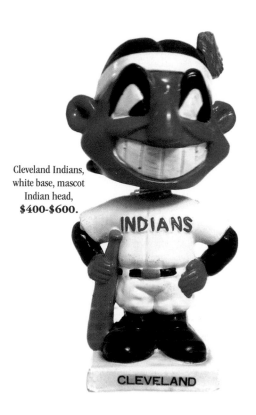

Cleveland Indians, white base, mascot Indian head, **$400-$600.**

Detroit Tigers, white base, mascot tiger head, **$225-$350.**

Houston Colt 45s, white base, mascot cowboy head, **$225-$350;**
and cowboy head with painted blue uniform, rare, **$600-$1,200.**

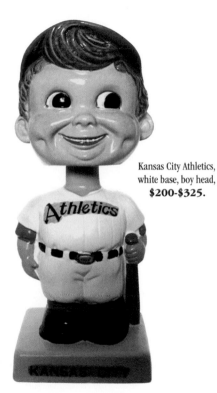

Kansas City Athletics,
white base, boy head,
**$200-$325.**

Los Angeles Angels,
white base, boy head,
**$150-$225.**

Los Angeles Dodgers, white base, boy head, decal across chest, **$125-$200;** and boy head, embossed lettering across chest, **$125-$200.**

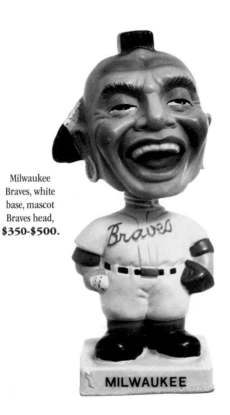

Milwaukee Braves, white base, mascot Braves head, **$350-$500.**

Minnesota Twins,
white base,
boy head,
**$1,000-$2,000.**

New York Mets, white base, boy head, two
uniform variations, **$300-$425.**

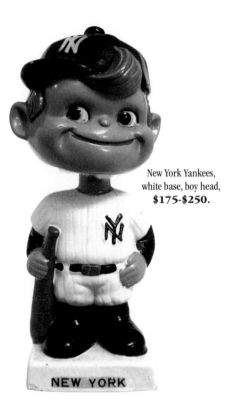

New York Yankees,
white base, boy head,
**$175-$250.**

Pittsburgh Pirates,
white base, mascot
pirate head,
**$500-$750.**

San Francisco Giants, white base, boy head, embossed lettering across chest, **$200-$325.**

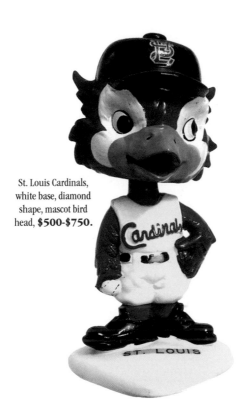

St. Louis Cardinals, white base, diamond shape, mascot bird head, **$500-$750.**

Washington Senators,
white base, boy head,
**$250-$375.**

Player dolls, Roberto Clemente, facsimile autograph decaled on base, rare doll, **$1,500-$2,500.**

Player dolls, Willie Mays, facsimile autograph decaled on base, can come with dark (on the left) or lighter features, **$450-$600.**

This is a rarer gold base variation of the Willie Mays player doll, **$450-$600.**

Mickey Mantle, round base and square base, **$650-$900.**

Roger Maris, facsimile autograph decaled on
base, two variations, **$450-$600.**

## 1961-1962 mini series

This series is almost an exact replica of the white base dolls except in miniature form. They measure about 4-1/2 inches tall and most are equipped with magnets under the base. Because of their size, they are logistically easier to display in a small area and have become extremely popular with collectors. The same nine mascot heads as the white base series were issued in this smaller version. There are several variations of boy head styles used for each team and each team was made with a doll carrying a bat and one with a ball and glove. Mantle and Maris were the only two "actual" player dolls produced. There are several unique variations in this series. The Cleveland Indians and Detroit Tigers can be found with both a white or green base. There is a rare version of the Baltimore Orioles doll with a boy head instead of the mascot bird head. The dolls can be found in individual generic boxes (worth about $25 each) or in set boxes of ten dolls for both the American and National Leagues (worth about $100 each). The Mantle and Maris dolls were originally sold in picture boxes that are now worth up to $100 each.

| Team | Variations/head style | EX/NM |
|------|----------------------|-------|
| Anaheim Angels | Paper label over the base decal, rare variation of Angels doll | $300/$500 |
| Baltimore Orioles | Mascot bird head (boy head $1,500) | $400/$600 |
| Boston Red Sox | Boy head | $275/$400 |
| Chicago Cubs | Mascot bear head | $600/$900 |
| Chicago White Sox | Boy head | $200/$325 |
| Cincinnati Reds | Mascot Mr. Redlegs head | $400/$600 |
| Cleveland Indians | Mascot Indian head | $400/$600 |
| Detroit Tigers | Mascot tiger head | $350/$500 |
| Houston Colt 45's | Mascot cowboy head | $225/$350 |
| Houston Astros | Mid-60s team issue* | $225/$350 |
| Los Angeles Angels | Boy head | $125/$200 |
| Los Angeles Dodgers | Boy head | $125/$200 |
| Kansas City Athletics | Boy head | $200/$325 |
| Milwaukee Braves | Mascot Braves head | $550/$800 |
| Minnesota Twins | Boy head | $200/$325 |
| Minneapolis Twins | Boy head | $600/$1,000 |
| New York Mets | Boy head, comes with dark blue or light blue uniform | $300/$425 |
| New York Yankees | Boy head | $175/$250 |
| Philadelphia Phillies | Boy head | $175/$250 |
| Pittsburgh Pirates | Mascot pirate head | $400/$600 |
| St. Louis Cardinals | Mascot bird head | $500/$750 |
| San Francisco Giants | Boy head | $250/$375 |
| Washington Senators | Boy head | $250/$375 |

**Player dolls**

| | | |
|------|----------------------|-------|
| Mickey Mantle | Facsimile autograph decaled on base, square or round base | $1,200/$2,000 |
| Roger Maris | Facsimile autograph decaled on base | $600/$800 |

*A later team issue.

Anaheim Angels, paper label over the base decal, rare variation, **$300-$500.**

Baltimore Orioles, mini, mascot bird head, **$400-$600;** and boy head, **$1,500.**

Chicago Cubs, mini, mascot bear head, **$600-$900.**

Cincinnati Reds, mini, mascot Mr. Redlegs head, **$400-$600.**

Cleveland Indians,
mini, mascot
Indian head,
**$400-$600.**

Detroit Tigers, mini, mascot tiger head, **$350-$500.**

Kansas City Athletics,
mini, boy head,
**$200-$325.**

Los Angeles Angels,
mini, boy head,
**$125-$200.**

Los Angeles Dodgers,
mini, boy head,
**$125-$200.**

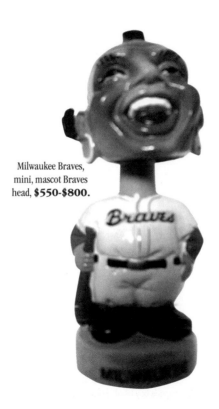

Milwaukee Braves,
mini, mascot Braves
head, **$550-$800.**

Minnesota Twins, mini, boy head, **$200-$325;** and a rarer
variation Minneapolis boy head, **$600-$1,000.**

New York Yankees,
mini, boy head,
**$175-$250.**

Philadelphia Phillies,
mini, boy head,
**$175-$250.**

Pittsburgh Pirates, mini, mascot pirate head, **$400-$600.**

San Francisco Giants,
mini, boy head,
**$250-$375.**

St. Louis Cardinals, mini, mascot bird head, **$500-$750.**

Mickey Mantle, mini, facsimile autograph decaled on
base, **$1,200-$2,000;** and original picture box the
Mickey Mantle mini doll was sold in, up to **$100.**

### 1963-1965 green base

Although most of the dolls are dated 1962 on the bottom of the base, it is the opinion of most that these dolls were not sold to the general public until 1963. All the dolls are on a round green base with the exception of the Orioles and Cardinals, which have diamond-shaped bases. There is a separate and harder to find series whose dolls have a square green base. The round green base series dolls are some of the most colorful and best made of any of the series. There are again nine mascot head dolls, but this series produced no actual player dolls. There are several hat color variations (Boston Red Sox and Kansas City As) that are a challenge to find. The Houston Colt 45 doll is unique in that he carries a "six-gun" in one hand. The dolls were originally sold in generic boxes that are now worth about $10.

This series has become increasingly popular because of its high quality and it is a more affordable alternative to the white base dolls. Do not confuse this series with the later heavy "ceramic" dolls made in Taiwan that also sport a green base.

| Team | Variations/head style | EX/NM |
|------|----------------------|-------|
| Anaheim Angels | Paper label over the base decal, rare variation of Angels doll | $300/$450 |
| Baltimore Orioles | Mascot bird head, diamond-shaped base | $150/$250 |
| Boston Red Sox | Boy head (red hat) | $100/$175 |
|  | Boy head (blue hat) | $200/$325 |
| Chicago Cubs | Mascot bear head | $300/$450 |
| Chicago White Sox | Boy head | $100/$150 |
| Cincinnati Reds | Mascot Mr. Redlegs head | $150/$225 |
| Cleveland Indians | Mascot Indian head | $200/$325 |
| Detroit Tigers | Mascot tiger head | $175/$250 |
| Houston Colt 45s | Mascot cowboy head, carries pistol | $350/$500 |
| Los Angeles Angels | Boy head | $100/$150 |
| Los Angeles Dodgers | Boy head | $100/$150 |
| Kansas City Athletics | Boy head (light blue hat) | $200/$300 |
|  | Boy head (dark blue hat) | $450/$700 |
| Milwaukee Braves | Mascot Braves head | $350/$500 |
| Minnesota Twins | Boy head | $150/$225 |
| New York Mets | Boy head | $100/$150 |
| New York Yankees | Boy head | $175/$250 |
| Philadelphia Phillies | Boy head | $100/$150 |
| Pittsburgh Pirates | Mascot pirate head | $175/$250 |
| St. Louis Cardinals | Mascot bird head, diamond-shaped base | $175/$250 |
| San Francisco Giants | Boy head | $100/$150 |
| Washington Senators | Boy head | $250/$375 |

Baltimore Orioles, green base, diamond shape, mascot bird head, **$150-$250.**

Boston Red Sox, green base, boy head, blue hat,
**$200-$325;** and red hat, **$100-$175.**

Chicago Cubs, green base, mascot bear head, **$300-$450.**

Cincinnati Reds,
green base, mascot
Mr. Redlegs head,
**$150-$225.**

Cleveland Indians,
green base, mascot
Indian head,
**$200-$325.**

Detroit Tigers,
green base,
mascot tiger head,
**$175-$250.**

Houston Colt 45s, green base, mascot cowboy head, carries pistol, **$350-$500.**

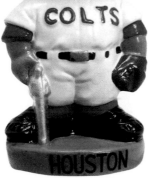

Kansas City Athletics, green base, boy head, dark blue hat,
**$450-$700;** and light blue hat, **$200-$300.**

Los Angeles Angels,
green base, boy head,
**$100-$150.**

Los Angeles Dodgers,
green base, boy head,
**$100-$150.**

Minnesota
Twins, green
base, boy head,
**$150-$225.**

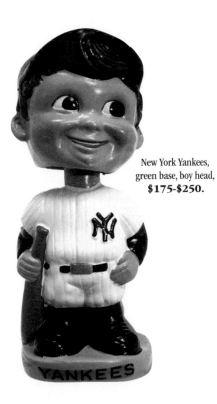

New York Yankees,
green base, boy head,
**$175-$250.**

Philadelphia Phillies,
green base, boy head,
**$100-$150.**

Pittsburgh Pirates,
green base, mascot
pirate head,
**$175-$250.**

San Francisco Giants,
green base, boy
head, **$100-$150.**

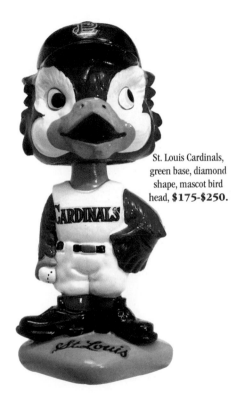

St. Louis Cardinals,
green base, diamond
shape, mascot bird
head, **$175-$250.**

Washington Senators,
green base, boy head,
**$250-$375.**

## 1963-1965 black face

This series is one of the finest looking and most desirable. Because of the "racial" climate of the country in the early 1960s, not many of the African-American dolls were produced or sold. Only 16 of the then 20 Major League teams are represented in this series (there is no Kansas City As, Minnesota Twins, Pittsburgh Pirates or San Francisco Giants). The dolls come on a round green base (Cubs can be round or square) and have two different style of boy faces (happy and serious). There is no particular premium for either face style, but the serious face seems to be more desired. All the dolls in this series are considered rare, with special difficulty in finding the Houston Colt 45, considered by many to be the "Holy Grail" of the hobby. The Colt 45s' black face has sold for as much as $11,000 in auction. These dolls usually suffer from condition problems on the rims of their heads. Be prepared to pay some serious money should you decide to collect them.

| Team | Variations/ head style | EX/NM | Team | Variations/ head style | EX/NM |
|------|------------------------|-------|------|------------------------|-------|
| Baltimore Orioles | Boy head | $850/$1,200 | L.A. Angels | Boy head | $1,000/$1,500 |
| | | | L.A. Dodgers | Boy head | $750/$1,000 |
| Boston Red Sox | Boy head | $1,000/$1,500 | Milwaukee Braves | Boy head | $1,000/$1,500 |
| Chicago Cubs | Boy head | $850/$1,200 | New York Mets | Boy head | $1,000/$1,500 |
| Chicago White Sox | Boy head | $750/$1,000 | New York Yankees | Boy head | $2,000/$3,000 |
| Cincinnati Reds | Boy head | $1,000/$1,500 | Philadelphia Phillies | Boy head | $850/$1,200 |
| Cleveland Indians | Boy head | $1,200/$1,750 | St. Louis Cardinals | Boy head | $750/$1,000 |
| Detroit Tigers | Boy head | $850/$1,200 | Washington Senators | Boy head | $750/$1,000 |
| Houston Colt 45s | Boy head, holding pistol in one hand | $5,000/$7,500 | | | |

Baltimore Orioles,
black face, boy head,
**$850-$1,200.**

Boston Red Sox,
black face, boy head,
**$1,000-$1,500.**

Chicago Cubs, black
face, boy head,
**$850-$1,200.**

Chicago White Sox,
black face, boy head,
**$750-$1,000.**

Cincinnati Reds,
black face, boy head,
**$1,000-$1,500.**

Cleveland Indians,
black face, boy head,
**$1,200-$1,750.**

Detroit Tigers, black
face, boy head,
**$850-$1,200.**

Houston Colt 45s,
black face, boy
head, holding
pistol in one hand,
**$5,000-$7,500.**

Los Angeles Angels,
black face, boy head,
**$1,000-$1,500.**

Los Angeles Dodgers,
black face, boy head,
**$750-$1,000.**

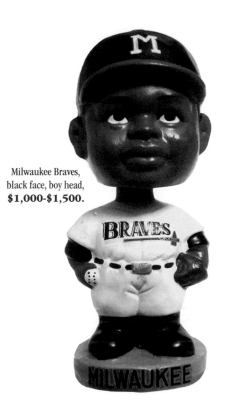

Milwaukee Braves,
black face, boy head,
**$1,000-$1,500.**

New York Mets, black face, boy head, two variations, **$1,000-$1,500.**

New York Yankees,
black face, boy head,
**$2,000-$3,000.**

Philadelphia Phillies,
black face, boy head,
**$850-$1,200.**

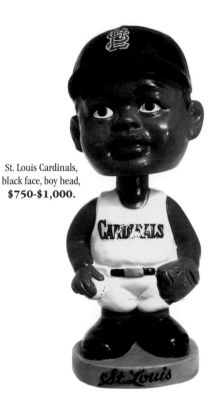

St. Louis Cardinals,
black face, boy head,
**$750-$1,000.**

Washington Senators,
black face, boy head,
**$750-$1,000**.

## 1966-1971 gold base

This is the last comprehensive series of the original baseball papier-mâché dolls. Due to the expansion of baseball and the moving of several teams to different cities, this series produced nine new team dolls that were not in the previous sets. Unfortunately, the gold base dolls are of inferior quality and although they are relatively plentiful, finding them in collectible condition can be a problem. They often suffer from flaking paint, chipped heads and decal wear. There are several harder to find variations in this series that make it a challenge to complete. With the inclusion of Mr. Met and the Texas Rangers, this series has 10 mascot head dolls. There is a rare Willie Mays gold base doll that is also generally included in this series. The dolls were again sold in generic boxes (except for the Mr. Met picture box worth about $75) that are worth about $10.

| Team | Variations/head style | EX/NM |
|------|----------------------|-------|
| Atlanta Braves | Mascot head, first doll in Braves new city | $125/$200 |
| Baltimore Orioles | Mascot bird head, diamond-shaped base | $125/$200 |
| Boston Red Sox | Boy head | $150/$225 |
| California Angels | Boy head, new city | $100/$150 |
| Chicago Cubs | Mascot bear head | $150/$225 |
| Chicago White Sox | Boy head | $85/$125 |
| Cincinnati Reds | Mascot Mr. Redlegs head | $150/$225 |
| Cleveland Indians | Mascot Indian head | $200/$300 |
| Detroit Tigers | Mascot tiger head | $150/$225 |
| Houston Astros | Boy head (blue hat), first doll with Astro name | $85/$12 |
| Houston Astros | Red hat, shooting star decal on chest, rare | $800/$1,000 |
| Los Angeles Dodgers | Boy head | $85/$125 |
| Kansas City Athletics | Boy head (green and gold uniform), hard to find doll | $600/$900 |
| Kansas City Royals | Boy head, new expansion team | $85/$125 |
| Milwaukee Brewers | Boy head, moved from Seattle | $85/$125 |
| Minnesota Twins | Boy head | $200/$325 |
| Montreal Expos | Boy head, new expansion team | $85/$125 |
| New York Mets | Boy head | $85/$125 |
| New York Mets | Mr. Met mascot head, bank and non bank variations | $300/$450 |
| New York Yankees | Boy head | $150/$225 |
| Oakland As | Boy head (yellow uniform, very common) | $75/$100 |
| Oakland As | Boy head (white uniform, white shoes) | $175/$250 |
| Philadelphia Phillies | Boy head | $85/$125 |
| Pittsburgh Pirates | Mascot pirate head | $150/$225 |
| St. Louis Cardinals | Mascot bird head, diamond-shaped base | $150/$225 |
| San Diego Padres | Boy head, new expansion team | $100/$150 |
| San Francisco Giants | Boy head | $100/$150 |
| Seattle Pilots | Boy head, one-year expansion team, rare | $300/$450 |
| Texas Rangers | Mascot Cowboy head, moved from Washington | $125/$200 |
| Washington Senators | Boy head (several hat variations) | $250/$375 |

**Player dolls**

| | | |
|------|----------------------|-------|
| Willie Mays | Gold base, #24 decaled on back, correct spelling of Mays | $800/$1,200 |

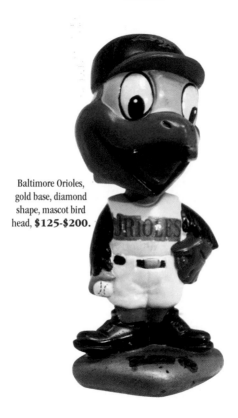

Baltimore Orioles, gold base, diamond shape, mascot bird head, **$125-$200.**

Chicago Cubs, gold base, mascot bear head, **$150-$225.**

Chicago White Sox, gold base, boy head, **$85-$125.**

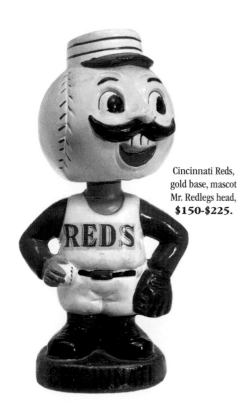

Cincinnati Reds, gold base, mascot Mr. Redlegs head, **$150-$225.**

Cleveland Indians,
gold base, mascot
Indian head,
**$200-$300.**

Detroit Tigers,
gold base, mascot
tiger head,
**$150-$225.**

Houston Astros, gold base, boy head (blue hat), first doll
with Astro name, **$85-$125;** and boy head, red hat,
shooting star decal on chest, rare, **$800-$1,000.**

Kansas City Athletics, gold base, boy head, green and gold uniform, hard to find doll, **$600-$900.**

Kansas City Royals,
gold base, boy head,
new expansion team,
**$85-$125.**

Los Angeles Dodgers,
gold base, boy head,
**$85-$125.**

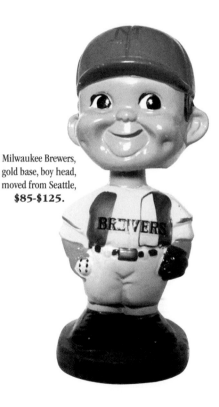

Milwaukee Brewers, gold base, boy head, moved from Seattle, **$85-$125.**

Minnesota Twins,
gold base, boy head,
**$200-$325.**

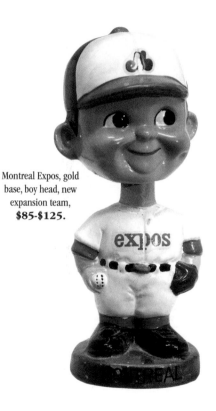

Montreal Expos, gold base, boy head, new expansion team, **$85-$125.**

New York Mets, gold base, boy head, **$85-$125;** and Mr. Met
mascot head, bank and non-bank variations, **$300-$450.**

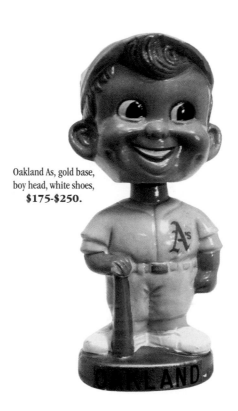

Oakland As, gold base,
boy head, white shoes,
**$175-$250.**

Philadelphia Phillies,
gold base, boy head,
**$85-$125.**

Pittsburgh Pirates, gold base, mascot pirate head, **$150-$225.**

San Diego Padres,
gold base, boy head,
new expansion team,
**$100-$150.**

St. Louis Cardinals, gold base, diamond shape, mascot bird head, **$150-$225.**

Texas Rangers, gold base, mascot cowboy head, moved from Washington, **$125-$200.**

Washington Senators, gold base, boy head (several color hat variations), **$250-$375.**

## 1970-1972 wedge base

This is the last of the "Golden Age" baseball dolls made of papier-mâché. This series is not popular with collectors because it has only eight Major League teams represented and no mascot dolls. The bases are square with rounded corners that feature different colors. Many collectors have been fooled by the Astros doll with the "orange hat" and "shooting star" decal, thinking it is from the gold base series. The dolls from this series are not particularly well made.

| Team | Variations/head style/base color | EX/NM |
|---|---|---|
| Boston Red Sox | Boy head, gold base | $200/$300 |
| California Angels | Boy head, white base | $100/$150 |
| Chicago Cubs | Boy head, green base | $200/$275 |
| Houston Astros | Boy head, gold base (blue hat) | $150/$200 |
| Houston Astros | Boy head, gold base (orange hat) | $150/$200 |
| Kansas City Royals | Boy head, gold base | $200/$300 |
| Minnesota Twins | Boy head, green base | $100/$150 |
| St. Louis Cardinals | Boy head, green base | $150/$200 |
| San Francisco Giants | Boy head, green base | $200/$300 |
| Denver Bears | Boy head, gold base, Minor League team | $400/$600 |

California Angels,
wedge base,
white, boy head,
**$100-$150.**

## 1960s team-issued dolls and rogue dolls

There are a number of dolls that appear to be limited edition dolls for particular teams. They were either sold at the home team's stadium or give-away promotions at special games. Because of their interesting designs, advanced collectors have become especially interested in these dolls. There are quite a number of generic baseball player and umpire dolls.

## Mid-1960s L.A. Dodgers and S.F. Giants Weirdo dolls

These incredible dolls have become one of the hottest series in the hobby. The Weirdo dolls each have different faces with hysterical expressions. They have either Dodgers or Giants emblazoned across their chests with their hats and uniforms in team colors. The dolls came with either a comical base decal or hang tag (very rare). There are seven known variations to the Dodgers Weirdo dolls with two of the variations coming with black faces. The Giants Weirdos were made with the same faces, but I have seen only three of them in over 20 years of collecting/ dealing. Mint examples of the Dodger Weirdos have sold from $1,000 to $5,500 over the past several years. The only two examples of the Giants Weirdos have sold for $3,500 and $5,000. They are all considered rare.

Mid-1960s Los Angeles Dodgers Weirdo dolls, with bather, **$1,000-$5,500;** and crybaby, **$1,000-$5,500.**

Mid-1960s Los Angeles Dodgers Weirdo dolls, sweeper,
two variations, **$1,000-$5,500.**

Mid-1960s Los Angeles Dodgers Weirdo dolls, grouchy,
**$1,000-$5,500;** and stealing base, **$1,000-$5,500.**

Mid-1960s Los Angeles Dodgers Weirdo dolls, two variations
of a screw in the baseball, **$1,000-$5,500.**

Mid-1960s San Francisco Giants Weirdo dolls, "Nice
Guys Always Finish last," **$1,000-$5,500.**

## Other oddball dolls

There are a number of different umpire dolls that fit in perfectly with almost every series of vintage baseball dolls. Some are not easy to find and can command hefty prices. The green-based umpire with balloon chest protector can bring as much as $1,500 in mint condition. Dolls issued by certain teams are also popular. Besides the Dodger Weirdo dolls, there are several other dolls that are specific to the L.A. Dodgers. There is a "Realistic faced" series of three (commonly referred to as the Don Drysdale series) that features a pitcher, batter and catcher. These dolls are fairly rare and can sell for as much as $500 each. A round white base boy pitcher with Dodgers decaled across his chest sells for about $150 and there is a larger L.A. Dodgers bobbing head bank that can fetch $200. The Houston Astros issued a large and mini white base doll shortly after their move to the Astrodome. Both dolls sell in the $175-$325 range. There are also team-issued dolls of the Boston Red Sox, N.Y. Yankees, L.A. Angels, Minnesota Twins and several minor league franchises.

Other oddball baseball dolls, green-based umpire with balloon chest protector, **$1,500 in mint condition.**

## Newer issues of baseball dolls

There were several series of baseball bobbing heads issued shortly after the "Golden Age." Although some of them are more than 30 years old, to most hardcore vintage doll collectors they are considered new and much less desirable. I will only briefly touch upon these series and give an overview price range as there are no truly rare dolls in these series.

## 1970s bobbing heads

All the Major League teams were made in a plastic issue in the early '70s. They are still relatively common mint in the box. There are no mascot dolls, with all dolls having the same boy face. Dolls found mint in the box are worth about $45 each and loose from $15 to $20 each. There was a Hank Aaron doll issued in 1975 by the Milwaukee Brewers. It is almost always found with its box, and although quite nice looking, it only retails for about $50.

There were two ceramic dolls issued in the mid/late '70s that have gained some popularity among collectors: mascot head dolls of the Cleveland Indians and Pittsburgh Pirates. They both have gold bases that can fool the novice collector into thinking they are "Golden Age" dolls, but the tell tale sign is their yellow uniforms and heaviness. They still sell from $150-$200 each.

## 1980s bobbing heads

In the early '80s, a company named Twin Enterprises issued a comprehensive Major League baseball series made of a heavy ceramic composition. They all have green bases, so please do not confuse them with the "green base" papier-mâché issue of the early '60s. They came with the same compliment of mascot heads as the Golden Age series with all others having the same boy face style. They can come either holding a bat or ball (a ball is harder to find) and they range in price from $30-$75. Twin Enterprises issued a slightly larger sized series in the mid- to late-'80s, which usually sell in the $25-$30 range.

An independent maker out of Minnesota issued a limited edition series of old-time player dolls in the late '80s. There were five baseball players and one football player in what was called the "Golden Era" dolls. The five baseball players produced were Babe Ruth, Lou Gehrig, Ty Cobb, Joe Jackson and Honus Wagner, with Bronco Nagurski being the lone football doll. They all sell for about $50 each with their boxes.

## 1990s to present day bobbing heads

There has been a rash of dolls issued since the bobbing head craze started again in the early '90s. Twins Enterprises issued yet another series (some wearing catcher's equipment) that generally sell for about $25-$30 each. Another company named Sam's flooded the hobby with dozens of actual player dolls. At first these dolls were extremely popular, but prices have leveled off and except for a few more desirable players, these dolls can be found in the $35-$50 range.

Major League and Minor League franchises have started incorporating actual player dolls as stadium give-aways. These dolls are limited to the amount given out during the promotion and in some cases have become extremely collectible. For the most part, though, they can usually be bought on the secondary market for about $25.

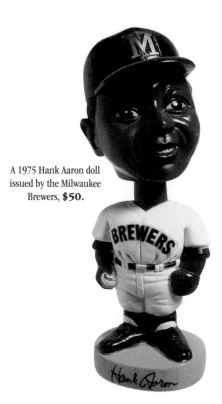

A 1975 Hank Aaron doll
issued by the Milwaukee
Brewers, **$50.**

Newer issue baseball doll, Gary Carter, New York Mets, **$35-$50.**

Newer issue baseball doll,
Ken Griffey Jr., Seattle
Mariners, **$35-$50.**

Newer issue baseball doll, Buddy Harrelson, Long
Island Ducks, two variations, **$25.**

Newer issue baseball doll, Michael Jordan, New York Rangers, **$35-$50.**

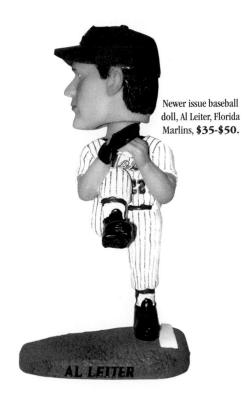

Newer issue baseball doll, Al Leiter, Florida Marlins, **$35-$50.**

Newer issue baseball doll, Mike Piazza, New York Mets, **$35-$50.**

Newer issue baseball doll, Carl Ripken Jr., Baltimore Orioles, **$35-$50.**

Newer issue baseball
doll, Babe Ruth,
**$50 with box.**

Newer issue baseball doll, Sammy Sosa, Chicago Cubs, **$35-$50.**

Another newer issue Sammy Sosa doll, **$35-$50.**

# Basketball Bobbing Heads

The National Basketball Association did not enjoy the same popularity in the 1960s as it did in the mid-1980s when stars like Larry Bird, Magic Johnson and, of course, Michael Jordan joined the league. Attendance was not high, so therefore the need for large amounts of souvenirs wasn't necessary. There were not many bobbing heads issued during the Golden Age of the hobby. In the early 1960s, only two NBA dolls were produced: a square-based New York Knicks and the Los Angeles Lakers. There were also two Harlem Globetrotter dolls issued around the same time. A later 1960s series produced four NBA team dolls: L.A. Lakers, Seattle Sonics, Boston Celtics and San Diego Rockets. A New York Knicks jumbo bank made of a ceramic composition was sold in the early 1970s. There was also an interesting series of NBA dolls that are usually mentioned with bobbing heads. They were called "Lil Dribblers" and although technically not a bobbing head, they are made of a similar composition and remind most people of nodders. The ball is actually the only moving part, as it bounces up and down.

| Team | EX/NM | Team | EX/NM |
|------|-------|------|-------|
| Baltimore Bullets | | Lil Dribbler (black player) | $125/$150 |
| Lil Dribbler (white player) | $250/$350 | Detroit Pistons | |
| Lil Dribbler (black player) | $200/$250 | Lil Dribbler (white player) | $125/$150 |
| Boston Celtics (Celtics decaled on chest, no base decal) | $400/$500 | Lil Dribbler (black player) | $125/$150 |
| | | Harlem Globetrotters | |
| Chicago Bulls | | Blue base | $450/$600 |
| Lil Dribbler (white player) | $175/$200 | Green base | $350/$500 |
| | | Lil Dribbler | $125/$150 |

| Team | EX/NM | Team | EX/NM |
|------|-------|------|-------|
| Los Angeles Lakers | | Lil Dribbler (white player) | $35/$50 |
| Square green base | $450/$600 | Lil Dribbler (black player) | $35/$50 |
| Gold base (white player) | $65/$85 | Philadelphia 76'ers | |
| Gold base (black player) | $350/$500 | Lil Dribbler (white player) | $300/$350 |
| Milwaukee Bucks | | Lil Dribbler (black player) | $200/$250 |
| Lil Dribbler (white player) | $125/$150 | San Diego Rockets, gold base | $250/$300 |
| Lil Dribbler (black player) | $125/$150 | Seattle Sonics | |
| New York Knicks | | Gold base (white player) | $300/$350 |
| Square orange base | $450/$600 | Gold base (black player) | $350/$500 |
| Large bank (white or black player) | $50/$75 | | |

Boston Celtics, Celtics decaled on chest, no base decal, **$400-$500.**

Detroit Pistons,
Lil Dribbler,
black player,
**$125-$150.**

Harlem Globetrotters,
Lil Dribbler,
**$125-$150.**

Harlem Globetrotters, blue base,
**$450-$600**; green base, **$350-$500**.

Los Angeles Lakers, square green base,
**$450-$600;** gold base, white player, **$65-$85.**

New York Knicks,
square orange base,
**$450-$600.**

San Diego Rockets,
gold base,
**$250-$300.**

## Newer basketball bobbing heads

Again, there is not much to mention except for some nice super-star players. They are again issued from SAM's and team and regional issues. Pricing ranges from $25-$50.

A newer issue Harlem Globetrotter doll, **$25-$50.**

# Football Bobbing Heads

There were no less than 14 different series of National Football League and American Football League dolls issued from 1960 through 1970. Add to these series a number of Canadian Football League sets and a host of college football dolls and you have literally hundreds of football bobbing heads to choose from. The uniform and helmet color variations have made football dolls some of the most collectible in the hobby. The following will break down the different series, but here is a quick tip: within many of the series there can be several variations of each team.

## 1960-61 NFL promotional dolls

These "Promo" dolls measure an incredible 13 inches tall. They were not sold to the general public, but were used as "point of sale" advertising tools for the first series of NFL dolls. They have no bases. The team names are decaled across the chest and their helmets are either decaled or painted to match the team colors. All of the then 13 NFL teams (there is no Minnesota Vikings) were issued. Most advanced collectors agree that there are probably less than 50 total examples of these dolls that still exist. Many of the dolls were repainted to the Eagles colors after their 1960 World Championship. All are extremely rare, with auction prices bringing anywhere from $2,500 to $10,000 depending on the team and condition. If you get one in your lifetime, consider yourself lucky. It will surely be one of the feature dolls in your collection.

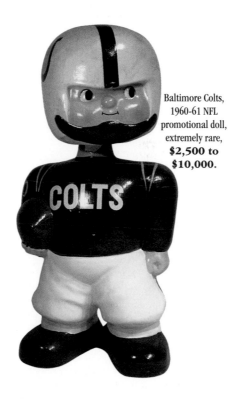

Baltimore Colts, 1960-61 NFL promotional doll, extremely rare, **$2,500 to $10,000.**

Cleveland Browns, 1960-61 NFL promotional doll, extremely rare, **$2,500 to $10,000.**

Detroit Lions, 1960-61 NFL promotional doll, extremely rare, **$2,500 to $10,000.**

Los Angeles Rams, 1960-61 NFL promotional doll, extremely rare, **$2,500 to $10,000.**

Philadelphia Eagles, 1960-61 NFL promotional doll, extremely rare, **$2,500 to $10,000.**

San Francisco
Forty-Niners, 1960-
61 NFL promotional
doll, extremely
rare, **$2,500
to $10,000.**

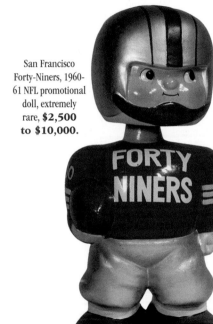

## 1960 NFL square base dolls

There are actually four separate and slightly different series that we group together because the same body type and head style is used for all. All of the dolls have co-coordinating base colors. The wood base series was first issued in 1960 and over the next three years, these dolls would sport either a plain papier-mâché base or one having "NFL" embossed on it. The other series is the "NFL" embossed with a black face. The black face dolls are always subject to scrutiny as many are repainted white dolls (be very careful buying these). Even though these are the earliest series of NFL dolls, with the exception of a few dolls and the black face variations, they were produced in large quantities and are not especially rare. They were all sold in generic plain boxes that add no real value.

| Team | Wood base | Square base | NFL embossed | Black face |
|---|---|---|---|---|
| Baltimore Colts | $75/$100 | $75/$100 | $75/$100 | $350/$500 |
| Chicago Bears | $100/$125 | $100/$125 | $125/$150 | $450/$600 |
| Cleveland Browns | $150/$200 | $150/$200 | $150/$200 | $750/$1,000 |
| Dallas Cowboys | $200/$250 (blue helmet) | $200/$250 | $250/$300 (white helmet) | $1,000/$1,500 |
| Detroit Lions | $75/$100 | $75/$100 | $125/$150 | $450/$600 |
| Green Bay Packers | $350/$500 | $150/$200 | $150/$200 | $750/$1,000 |
| Los Angels Rams | $75/$100 (blue uniform) $350/$500 (gold uniform) | $75/$100 | $125/$150 | $750/$1,000 |
| Minnesota Vikings | No doll issued | $150/$200 | $150/$200 | No doll issued |

| Team | Wood base | Square base | NFL embossed | Black face |
|------|-----------|-------------|--------------|------------|
| New York Giants | $125/$150 | $125/$150 | $125/$150 | $750/$1,000 |
| Philadelphia Eagles | $125/$150 | $125/$150 | $125/$150 | $350/$500 |
| Pittsburgh Steelers | $150/$200 | $150/$200 | $150/$200 | $750/$1,000 |
| St. Louis Cardinals | $75/$100 | $75/$100 | $75/$100 | $750/$1,000 |
| San Francisco Forty Niners | $75/$100 | $75/$100 | $75/$100 | $1,000/$1,500 |
| Washington Redskins | $200/$250 | $200/$250 | $200/$250 | $1,750/$2,000 |

Baltimore Colts, square base, **$75-$100;**
square base, black face, **$350-$500.**

Chicago Bears, square base, **$100-$125;** square
base, NFL embossed, **$125-$150.**

Chicago Bears,
square base, NFL
embossed, black face,
**$450-$600.**

Cleveland Browns, square base, **$150-$200;**
square base, NFL embossed, **$150-$200.**

Dallas Cowboys, square base, **$200-$250;** square
base, NFL embossed, **$200-$250.**

Dallas Cowboys,
square base, wooden,
blue helmet,
**$200-$250.**

Detroit Lions,
square base,
**$75-$100.**

Green Bay Packers, square base, **$150-$200;**
square base, NFL embossed, **$150-$200.**

Los Angeles Rams, square base, wooden, gold uniform,
**$350-$500;** square base, wooden, blue uniform, **$75-$100.**

Minnesota Vikings, square base, **$150-$200.**

New York Giants, square base, **$125-$150;**
square base, NFL embossed, **$125-$150.**

New York Giants,
square base,
NFL embossed,
black face,
**$750-$1,000.**

Philadelphia Eagles, square base, **$125-$150;**
square base, NFL embossed, **$125-$150.**

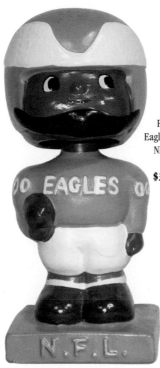

Philadelphia
Eagles, square base,
NFL embossed,
black face,
**$350-$500.**

Pittsburgh Steelers, square base, wooden,
**$150-$200**; square base, **$150-$200**.

Pittsburgh
Steelers,
square base,
NFL embossed,
**$150-$200**.

San Francisco Forty-Niners, square base,
**$75-$100**; square base, wooden, **$75-$100**.

San Francisco Forty-Niners, square base, NFL embossed, black face, **$1,000-$1,500.**

St. Louis Cardinals, square base, **$75-$100;**
square base, wooden, **$75-$100.**

St. Louis Cardinals,
square base,
NFL embossed,
black face,
**$750-$1,000.**

Washington Redskins, square base, **$200-$250;**
square base, NFL embossed, **$200-$250.**

Washington
Redskins,
square base, NFL
embossed, black
face, **$1,750-
$2,000.**

## 1961-62 AFL toes-up with baggy pants

This was the first issue of dolls of the fledgling AFL. There were only eight teams in the league and all had their own dolls. There are two variations for each team with the base colors differing from team to team. One variation has only the team nickname decaled on the base with a blank chest. The other variation has the team name on the chest and city name on the base. There is no premium for either, but for the hard-core collector, having both variations is a must. There is a sticker on the bottom of the base that reads "American Football League." Because of the rather large heads and poor quality, these dolls usually suffer condition problems, but they are still one of the most sought after football dolls in the hobby.

| Team | EX/NM |
|------|-------|
| Boston Patriots | $350/$500 |
| Buffalo Bills | $350/$500 |
| Dallas Texans | $1,000/$1,250 |
| Denver Broncos | $850/$1,000 |
| Houston Oilers | $850/$1,000 |
| New York Titans | $1,500/$2,000 |
| Oakland Raiders | $850/$1,000 |
| San Diego Chargers | $400/$600 |

Boston Patriots, 1961-62 AFL toes-up with baggy
pants, blue base, **$350-$500.**

Buffalo Bills, 1961-62 AFL toes-up with baggy pants,
blue base, two variations, each **$350-$500.**

Dallas Texans, 1961-62 AFL toes-up with baggy pants, gold
base, two variations, each **$1,000-$1,250.**

Denver Broncos, 1961-62 AFL toes-up with baggy pants, gold base, **$850-$1,000.**

Houston Oilers, 1961-62 AFL toes-up with baggy pants, white base,
light blue uniform, team name on chest, and a variation with
dark blue uniform and blank chest, each **$850-$1,000.**

Oakland Raiders, 1961-62 AFL toes-up with baggy pants, gold base, two variations, each **$850-$1,000.**

New York Titans,
1961-62 AFL
toes-up with
baggy pants,
**$1,500-
$2,000.**

San Diego
Chargers,
1961-62 AFL
toes-up with
baggy pants,
**$400-$600.**

## 1961-1966 NFL/AFL toes-up

This series may be the most confusing of all the doll sets. There are four completely different white face variations that are usually lumped together and it seems that no-one has a true grasp as to how many dolls were actually produced. There were 15 NFL teams that fall into this category and several dolls of AFL teams. The NFL series are generally grouped into four types, but even the experts agree that there may be other variations. I'll try to make it as easy as possible, but trust me, they are tough to describe. All the dolls in these series stand on round bases with their toes pointed up. There is a separate series of "Black Face Toes-up" NFL dolls that are extremely rare.

**Type 1** – 14 NFL teams represented (there is no Atlanta Falcons); ball held in a vertical position. The team name is embossed (raised lettering) across the chest. The city name is decaled on the base with smallish print, but some of the dolls may just have "N.F.L." embossed on the base. The base colors match the team colors.

**Type 2** – Again, the same 14 teams as the Type 1 dolls. This type is the easiest to detect as all stand on a round gold base with the ball being held vertically. The base decal (city) has larger lettering than Type 1, which can be in either script or block letters. The team name can be either decaled or embossed across the chest.

**Type 3** – Types 3 and 4 present the most problems for collectors. Type 3 dolls hold the ball horizontally. The bases are various colors and have the city decaled on it. Team names are decaled across the chest. The same 14 teams as Types 1 and 2 are represented.

**Type 4** – This type introduced a new team, the expansion Atlanta Falcons. The ball is held horizontally. The bases are all different colors with some matching the team colors. The city decals on the base can come large or small. The team names are decaled across the chest. There are some odd variations in this series. The Pittsburgh Steelers comes on a red base and the Baltimore Colts have the city spelled incorrectly (Balitmore). It is a very tough series to complete.

**Black Face NFL** – All are on round gold bases. The facial features are different from the "white face" dolls making them impossible to paint over. All are scarce.

**AFL Type** – There are several different AFL dolls that sport this "Toes-Up" style. There are five known dolls (Buffalo Bills, K.C. Chiefs, Denver Broncos, Houston Oilers and Oakland Raiders) that have numbers decaled on their chest. There are also "Toes-Up" examples of the Miami Dolphins and another Houston Oiler (with a white base). All the AFL "Toes-up" dolls are considered hard to find.

| Team | Type 1 | Type 2 | Type 3 | Type 4 $300/$500 | Black face No doll |
|------|--------|--------|--------|--------|--------|
| Atlanta Falcons | | | | $300/$500 | No doll |
| Baltimore Colts | $300/$500 | $300/$500 | $300/$450 | $500/$750 | $1,250/1,750 |
| Chicago Bears | $250/$350 | $200/$300 | $200/$300 | $400/$600 | $600/$900 |
| Cleveland Browns | $400/$600 | $250/$350 | $400/$600 | $500/$750 | $1,000/$1,500 |
| Dallas Cowboys | $400/$600 | $250/$350 | $250/$350 | $400/$600 | $1,500/$2,000 |
| Detroit Lions | $400/$600 | $300/$450 | $250/$350 | $400/$600 | $750/$1,000 |
| Green Bay Packers | $400/$600 | $250/$350 | $250/$350 | $400/$600 | $750/$1,000 |
| Los Angeles Rams | $200/$300 | $200/$300 | $200/$300 | $400/$600 | $600/$900 |
| Minnesota Vikings | $400/$600 | $200/$300 | $200/$300 | $400/$600 | $750/$1,000 |
| New York Giants | $400/$600 | $150/$225 | $150/$225 | $400/$600 | $600/$900 |
| Philadelphia Eagles | $300/$500 | $250/$350 | $200/$300 | $400/$600 | $600/$900 |
| Pittsburgh Steelers | $300/$500 | $200/$300 | $200/$300 | $600/$900 | $750/$1,000 |
| St. Louis Cardinals | $300/$500 | $200/$300 | $300/$450 | $250/$400 | None known |
| San Francisco Forty-Niners | $400/$600 | $300/$450 | $300/$450 | $400/$600 | $600/$900 |
| Washington Redskins | $500/$750 | $250/$350 | $250/$350 | $1,000/$1,500 | $2,000/$3,000 |

| AFL Teams | Various types | EX/NM |
|-----------|---------------|-------|
| Buffalo Bills | #31 on chest | $350/$500 |
| Denver Broncos | #62 on chest | $750/$1,000 |
| Houston Oilers | #10 on chest | $600/$800 |
| Houston Oilers | White base | $400/$600 |
| K.C. Chiefs | #55 on chest | $750/$1,000 |
| Oakland Raiders | #11 on chest (two known) | $2,000/$3,000 |
| Miami Dolphins | Gold base | $200/$300 |

Atlanta Falcons,
1961-66 NFL/AFL
toes-up, Type 4,
**$300-$500.**

Baltimore Colts,
1961-66 NFL/AFL
toes-up, Type 1,
**$300-$500.**

Baltimore Colts,
1961-66 NFL/AFL
toes-up, Type 4,
with Baltimore
misspelled
on base,
**$500-$750.**

Chicago Bears, 1961-66 NFL/AFL toes-up,
Type 1, two variations, **$250-$350.**

Chicago Bears, 1961-66 NFL/AFL toes-up, Type 2,
**$200-$300;** and black face, **$600-$900.**

Cleveland Browns, 1961-66 NFL/AFL toes-up,
Type 1, two variations, **$400-$600.**

Cleveland Browns,
1961-66 NFL/AFL
toes-up, Type 4,
**$500-$750.**

Dallas Cowboys, 1961-66 NFL/AFL toes-up, Type 1, left,
**$400-$600;** and Type 3, **$250-$350.**

Dallas Cowboys,
1961-66 NFL/AFL
toes-up, black face,
**$1,500-$2,000.**

Detroit Lions, 1961-66 NFL/AFL toes-up, Type 1, left,
**$400-$600;** and Type 4, **$400-$600.**

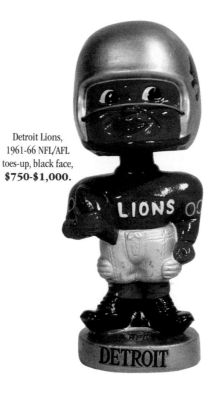

Detroit Lions,
1961-66 NFL/AFL
toes-up, black face,
**$750-$1,000.**

Houston Oilers,
1961-66 NFL/AFL
toes-up, Type
3, white base,
**$400-$600.**

Green Bay Packers, 1961-66 NFL/AFL toes-up, Type 1,
left, **$400-$600;** and Type 2, **$250-$350.**

Green Bay Packers, 1961-66 NFL/AFL toes-up, Type 4, **$400-$600.**

Los Angeles Rams, 1961-66 NFL/AFL toes-up, Type 1,
left, **$200-$300;** and Type 4, **$400-$600.**

Los Angeles
Rams, 1961-66
NFL/AFL toes-
up, black face,
**$600-$900.**

Minnesota Vikings, 1961-66 NFL/AFL toes-up, Type 2,
left, **$200-$300;** and Type 4, **$400-$600.**

Minnesota
Vikings, 1961-66
NFL/AFL toes-
up, black face,
**$750-$1,000.**

New York Giants, 1961-66 NFL/AFL toes-up, Type 1, left,
**$400-$600;** and Type 2, **$150-$225.**

New York Giants, 1961-66 NFL/AFL toes-up, Type 4,
**$400-$600;** and black face, **$600-$900.**

Philadelphia Eagles, 1961-66 NFL/AFL toes-up, Type 1,
left, **$300-$500;** and Type 4, **$400-$600.**

Philadelphia
Eagles, 1961-66
NFL/AFL toes-
up, black face,
**$600-$900.**

Pittsburgh Steelers, 1961-66 NFL/AFL toes-up, Type 1,
left, **$300-$500;** and Type 2, **$200-$300.**

Pittsburgh Steelers, 1961-66 NFL/AFL toes-up, Type 4, left,
**$600-$900;** and black face, **$750-$1,000.**

San Francisco Forty-Niners, 1961-66 NFL/AFL toes-up, black face, **$600-$900.**

St. Louis Cardinals, 1961-66 NFL/AFL toes-up, Type 1, left,
**$300-$500;**and Type 3, red base, **$300-$450.**

Washington Redskins, 1961-66 NFL/AFL toes-up, Type 1,
left, **$500-$750;** and Type 2, **$250-$350.**

Washington Redskins, 1961-66 NFL/AFL toes-up, Type 3, left,
**$250-$350;** and black face, **$2,000-$3,000.**

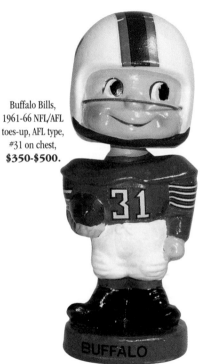

Buffalo Bills,
1961-66 NFL/AFL
toes-up, AFL type,
#31 on chest,
**$350-$500.**

Denver Broncos,
1961-66 NFL/AFL
toes-up, AFL type,
#62 on chest,
**$750-$1,000.**

Houston Oilers,
1961-66 NFL/AFL
toes-up, AFL type,
#10 on chest,
**$600-$800.**

Kansas City Chiefs,
1961-66 NFL/AFL
toes-up, AFL type,
#55 on chest,
**$750-$1,000.**

Miami Dolphins, 1961-66 NFL/AFL toes-up, AFL type, gold base, **$200-$300.**

Oakland Raiders,
1961-66 NFL/AFL
toes-up, AFL type,
#11 on chest
(two known),
**$2,000-
$3,000.**

## 1962-1964 NFL/AFL kissing pairs

Each of the then 14 NFL teams is represented (plus two AFL teams), with each set having an NFL player and a matching Majorette. Two of the teams (the Pittsburgh Steelers and Cleveland Browns) have mascot heads instead of the standard boy head. The dolls are equipped with magnets in their lips to simulate a kissing action. The city names are decaled on the base and the team name across the chest. All have round gold bases, with the exception of the Steelers—that stands on a base resembling a steel beam. There is some skepticism about the legitimacy of the AFL Kissers. They came in generic boxes that picture kissing dolls.

| Team | EX/NM |
|---|---|
| Baltimore Colts | $450/$600 |
| Chicago Bears | $450/$600 |
| Cleveland Browns (Brownie elf) | $1,000/$1,500 |
| Dallas Cowboys | $300/$400 |
| Detroit Lions | $500/$750 |
| Green Bay Packers | $450/$600 |
| Los Angeles Rams | $300/$400 |
| Minnesota Vikings | $300/$400 |
| New York Giants | $450/$600 |
| Philadelphia Eagles | $500/$750 |
| Pittsburgh Steelers (steel worker) | $750/$1,000 |
| St. Louis Cardinals | $300/$400 |
| San Francisco Forty-Niners | $450/$600 |
| Washington Redskins | $1,250/$1,750 |
| **AFL kissing pairs** | |
| Boston Patriots | $300/$400 |
| Buffalo Bills | $300/$400 |

Baltimore Colts, 1962-64 NFL/AFL kissing pairs, **$450-$600.**

Chicago Bears, 1962-64 NFL/AFL kissing pairs, **$450-$600.**

Cleveland Browns, 1962-64 NFL/AFL kissing pairs
with Brownie elf, **$1,000-$1,500.**

Dallas Cowboys, 1962-64 NFL/AFL kissing pairs, **$300-$400.**

Detroit Lions, 1962-64 NFL/AFL kissing pairs, **$500-$750.**

Green Bay Packers, 1962-64 NFL/AFL kissing pairs, **$450-$600.**

Los Angeles Rams, 1962-64 NFL/AFL kissing pairs, **$300-$400.**

Philadelphia Eagles, 1962-64 NFL/AFL kissing pairs, **$500-$750.**

Minnesota Vikings, 1962-64 NFL/AFL kissing pairs, **$300-$400.**

New York Giants, 1962-64 NFL/AFL kissing pairs, **$450-$600.**

Pittsburgh Steelers, 1962-64 NFL/AFL kissing pairs
with steel worker, **$750-$1,000.**

San Francisco Forty-Niners, 1962-64 NFL/
AFL kissing pairs, **$450-$600.**

St. Louis Cardinals, 1962-64 NFL/AFL kissing pairs, **$300-$400.**

Washington Redskins, 1962-64 NFL/AFL
kissing pairs, **$1,250-$1,750.**

## 1963-1964 NFL square gold base

Because only seven of the then 14 NFL teams were produced in the series, it is not particularly popular among collectors. All the dolls stand on a square gold base with either the city name decaled or N.F.L. embossed on the base. Several of the teams were made with black faces.

| Team | EX/NM |
|---|---|
| Baltimore Colts | $300/$400 |
| Baltimore Colts (black player) | $500/$750 |
| Chicago Bears | $250/$300 |
| Detroit Lions | $500/750 |
| Detroit Lions (black player, only one known example) | $1,000/$1,500 |
| Minnesota Vikings | $350/$500 |
| New York Giants | $350/$500 |
| St. Louis Cardinals | $350/$500 |
| St. Louis Cardinals (black player) | $350/$500 |
| Washington Redskins | $350/$500 |

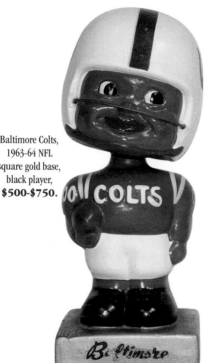

Baltimore Colts,
1963-64 NFL
square gold base,
black player,
**$500-$750.**

Chicago Bears,
1963-64 NFL
square gold base,
**$250-$300.**

Detroit Lions,
1963-64 NFL
square gold
base, black
player, only one
known example,
**$1,000-
$1,500.**

Minnesota Vikings, 1963-64 NFL square gold base, **$350-$500.**

New York Giants,
1963-64 NFL
square gold base,
**$350-$500.**

St. Louis Cardinals,
1963-64 NFL
square gold base,
black player,
**$350-$500.**

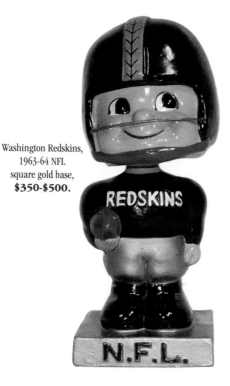

Washington Redskins,
1963-64 NFL
square gold base,
**$350-$500.**

## 1965-1966 AFL Earpads

This series is quickly becoming one of the most popular of all the football series. The helmet somewhat resembles a "space helmet" with earpads that stick out of each side. All the dolls stand on a round gold base. The helmets have great looking decals on each side and the dolls are extremely colorful. There are only the nine existing AFL teams and one rogue NFL doll, the very rare Washington Redskins.

| Team | EX/NM |
|---|---|
| Boston Patriots | $350/$500 |
| Buffalo Bills | $350/$500 |
| Denver Broncos | $1,500/$2,000 |
| Kansas City Chiefs | $300/$400 |
| Houston Oilers | $500/$750 |
| Miami Dolphins | $500/$750 |
| New York Jets | $750/$1,000 |
| Oakland Raiders | $1,000/$1,250 |
| San Diego Chargers | $400/$600 |
| Washington Redskins (only known NFL team in the series) | $2,000/$2,500 |

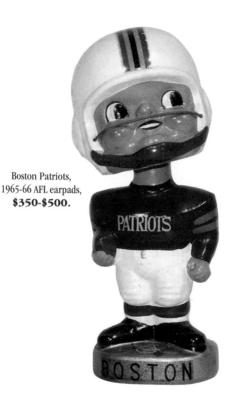

Boston Patriots,
1965-66 AFL earpads,
**$350-$500.**

Buffalo Bills,
1965-66 AFL
earpads, **$350-
$500**.

Denver Broncos, 1965-66 AFL earpads, **$1,500-$2,000.**

Houston Oilers,
1965-66 AFL
earpads,
**$500-$750.**

Kansas City
Chiefs, 1965-66
AFL earpads,
**$300-$400.**

Miami Dolphins,
1965-66 AFL earpads,
**$500-$750.**

New York Jets,
1965-66 AFL earpads,
**$750-$1,000.**

Oakland Raiders,
1965-66 AFL
earpads, **$1,000-
$1,250.**

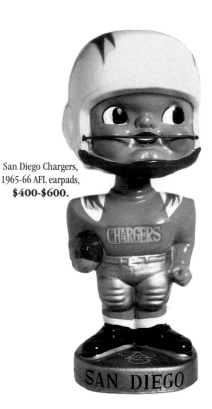

San Diego Chargers,
1965-66 AFL earpads,
**$400-$600.**

Washington
Redskins, only
known NFL team
doll with earpads,
**$2,000-$2,500.**

## 1965-1967 AFL/NFL round gold base

This is a wonderful series of football dolls. They all stand on a round gold base. All the NFL teams were made and over the last few years there has been the discovery of several AFL teams that were not catalogued before. A word of caution: these dolls look similar to the Merger series of 1968-1970 featured later in the book. The facial features and body types are quite similar, but upon close inspection, you will notice the differences.

| Team NFL | EX/NM |
|---|---|
| Atlanta Falcons | $100/$125 |
| Baltimore Colts | $150/$200 |
| Chicago Bears | $150/$200 |
| Cleveland Browns | $250/$300 |
| Dallas Cowboys | $300/$375 |
| Detroit Lions | $150/$200 |
| Green Bay Packers | $250/$300 |
| Los Angeles Rams | $400/$600 |
| Minnesota Vikings | $300/$400 |
| New Orleans Saints | $100/$125 |
| New York Giants | $150/$200 |
| Philadelphia Eagles | $200/$250 |
| Pittsburgh Steelers | $250/$300 |
| St. Louis Cardinals | $250/$300 |
| San Francisco Forty-Niners | $450/$600 |
| Washington Redskins | $300/$375 |

| Team AFL | EX/NM |
|---|---|
| Denver Broncos | $500/$750 |
| Houston Oilers | $400/$600 |
| Kansas City Chiefs | $500/$750 |
| Oakland Raiders | $500/$750 |

Atlanta Falcons,
1965-67 AFL/NFL
round gold base,
**$100-$125.**

Baltimore Colts,
1965-67 AFL/NFL
round gold base,
**$150-$200.**

Chicago Bears,
1965-67 AFL/NFL
round gold base,
**$150-$200.**

Cleveland Browns,
1965-67 AFL/NFL
round gold base,
**$250-$300.**

Dallas Cowboys,
1965-67 AFL/NFL
round gold base,
**$300-$375.**

Denver Broncos,
1965-67 AFL/NFL
round gold base,
**$500-$750.**

Detroit Lions,
1965-67 AFL/NFL
round gold base,
**$150-$200.**

Green Bay Packers,
1965-67 AFL/NFL
round gold base,
**$250-$300.**

Houston Oilers,
1965-67 AFL/NFL
round gold base,
**$400-$600.**

Kansas City
Chiefs, 1965-67
AFL/NFL round
gold base,
**$500-$750.**

Los Angeles Rams,
1965-67 AFL/NFL
round gold base,
**$400-$600.**

Philadelphia Eagles,
1965-67 AFL/NFL
round gold base,
**$200-$250.**

Minnesota Vikings,
1965-67 AFL/NFL
round gold base,
**$300-$400.**

New York Giants,
1965-67 AFL/NFL
round gold base,
**$150-$200.**

New Orleans
Saints, 1965-67
AFL/NFL round
gold base,
**$100-$125.**

Oakland Raiders,
1965-67 AFL/NFL
round gold base,
**$500-$750.**

Pittsburgh Steelers,
1965-67 AFL/NFL
round gold base,
**$250-$300.**

San Francisco
Forty-Niners,
1965-67 AFL/NFL
round gold base,
**$450-$600.**

St. Louis Cardinals,
1965-67 AFL/NFL
round gold base,
**$250-$300.**

Washington
Redskins, 1965-67
AFL/NFL round gold
base, **$300-$375.**

## 1965-1967 NFL realistic face

This series is the first to institute a more mature realistic looking face as opposed to the traditional "boy" faced dolls. Only 12 of the then 16 NFL teams were issued and again they all stand on a round gold base.

| Team NFL | EX/NM |
|----------|-------|
| Atlanta Falcons | $125/$150 |
| Baltimore Colts | $600/$800 |
| Chicago Bears | $200/$250 |
| Cleveland Browns | $400/$500 |
| Dallas Cowboys | $600/$800 |
| Detroit Lions | $300/$400 |
| Green Bay Packers | $300/$400 |
| Minnesota Vikings | $500/$750 |
| New Orleans Saints | $100/$125 |
| Philadelphia Eagles | $250/$300 |
| St. Louis Cardinals | $150/$200 |
| Washington Redskins | $1,200/$1,500 |

Atlanta Falcons,
1965-67 NFL
realistic face,
**$125-$150.**

Chicago Bears,
1965-67 NFL
realistic face,
**$200-$250.**

Cleveland Browns,
1965-67 NFL
realistic face,
**$400-$500**

Dallas Cowboys,
1965-67 NFL
realistic face,
**$600-$800.**

Detroit Lions,
1965-67 NFL
realistic face,
**$300-$400.**

Green Bay Packers,
1965-67 NFL
realistic face,
**$300-$400.**

New Orleans Saints, 1965-67 NFL realistic face, **$100-$125.**

Philadelphia
Eagles, 1965-67
NFL realistic face,
**$250-$300.**

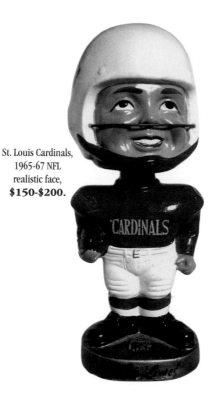

St. Louis Cardinals,
1965-67 NFL
realistic face,
**$150-$200.**

Washington Redskins, 1965-67 NFL realistic face, **$1,200-$1,500.**

# 1968-1970 NFL/AFL Merger Series

This series is probably the most recognizable among the "Baby Boomer" generation. Because of the impending and subsequent merger of the NFL and the AFL, this series is the most comprehensive of all the football series. All 26 of the then professional American football franchises were represented with several of the teams having a number of uniform variations. All the dolls stand on a round gold base (remember not to confuse this with the 1965 gold base series). A number of the original AFL teams may have "AFL" decals between their feet, but all the teams also come with NFL decals.

| Team | EX/NM | Team | EX/NM |
|------|-------|------|-------|
| Atlanta Falcons (red jersey) | $100/$125 | Kansas City Chiefs | $65/$85 |
| Atlanta Falcons (black jersey) | $200/$250 | Los Angeles Rams | $100/$125 |
| | | Los Angeles Rams (gold horns) | $250/$300 |
| Baltimore Colts | $150/$200 | | |
| Boston Patriots (see New England Patriots) | $200/$250 | Miami Dolphins | $200/$250 |
| | | Minnesota Vikings | $150/$200 |
| Buffalo Bills | $250/$300 | New England Patriots | $150/$200 |
| Chicago Bears | $150/$200 | New Orleans Saints | $100/$125 |
| Cincinnati Bengals | $85/$100 | N. O. Saints (black helmet) | $200/$250 |
| Cleveland Browns | $200/$250 | New York Giants | $85/$100 |
| Dallas Cowboys (blue helmet) | $200/$250 | New York Jets | $125/$150 |
| | | Oakland Raiders | $150/$200 |
| Dallas Cowboys (silver helmet) | $200/$250 | Philadelphia Eagles | $150/$200 |
| | | P. Eagles (green wings) | $175/$225 |
| Denver Broncos (red jersey) | $200/$250 | Pittsburgh Steelers | $250/$300 |
| Denver Broncos (blue jersey) | $250/$300 | St. Louis Cardinals | $65/$85 |
| Detroit Lions | $65/$85 | San Diego Chargers | $150/$200 |
| Green Bay Packers | $250/$300 | San Francisco Forty-Niners | $150/$200 |
| Houston Oilers (silver helmet) | $85/$100 | S.F. Forty Niners (white helmet) | $250/$300 |
| Houston Oilers (blue helmet) | $150/$200 | Washington Redskins (four variations) | $200/$250 |

Atlanta Falcons, 1968-1970 NFL/AFL merger series, two uniform
variations, red jersey, shown, **$100-$125;** black jersey, **$200-$250.**

Baltimore Colts, 1968-1970 NFL/AFL merger series, **$150-$200.**

Buffalo Bills, 1968-1970 NFL/AFL merger series, **$250-$300.**

Chicago Bears, 1968-1970 NFL/AFL merger series, **$150-$200.**

Cincinnati Bengals,
1968 1970 NFL/AFL
merger series,
**$85-$100.**

Cleveland Browns,
1968-1970 NFL/AFL
merger series,
**$200-$250.**

Dallas Cowboys, 1968-1970 NFL/AFL merger series, blue
helmet, **$200-$250;** and silver helmet, **$200-$250.**

Denver Broncos, 1968-1970 NFL/AFL merger series, doll with blue
jersey, **$250-$300;** doll with red jersey, **$200-$250.**

Detroit Lions,
1968-1970 NFL/AFL
merger series,
**$65-$85.**

Green Bay Packers,
1968-1970 NFL/AFL
merger series,
**$250-$300.**

Houston Oilers, 1968-1970 NFL/AFL merger series, silver helmet,
**$85-$100;** and blue helmet (not shown), **$150-$200.**

Kansas City Chiefs,
1968-1970 NFL/AFL
merger series,
**$65-$85.**

Los Angeles Rams, 1968-1970 NFL/AFL merger series, doll at left,
**$100-$125;** doll at right with gold horns, **$250-$300.**

Miami Dolphins, 1968-1970 NFL/AFL merger series, **$200-$250.**

Minnesota Vikings,
1968-1970 NFL/AFL
merger series,
**$150-$200.**

New England Patriots, left, 1968-1970 NFL/AFL merger series,
**$150-$200;** doll at right, Boston Patriots, **$200-$250.**

New Orleans Saints, 1968-1970 NFL/AFL merger series, doll at left
with black helmet, **$200-$250;** doll at right, **$100-$125.**

New York Giants,
1968-1970 NFL/AFL
merger series,
**$85-$100.**

New York Jets,
1968-1970 NFL/AFL
merger series,
**$125-$150.**

Oakland Raiders,
1968-1970 NFL/AFL
merger series,
**$150-$200.**

Philadelphia Eagles, 1968-1970 NFL/AFL merger series, doll on left with green wings on helmet, **$175-$225;** doll at right, **$150-$200.**

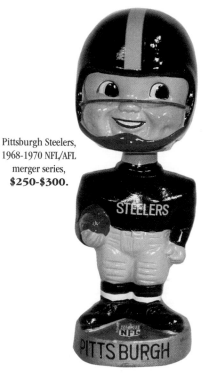

Pittsburgh Steelers,
1968-1970 NFL/AFL
merger series,
**$250-$300.**

San Diego Chargers,
1968-1970 NFL/AFL
merger series,
**$150-$200.**

San Francisco 49ers, 1968-1970 NFL/AFL merger series, doll with
white helmet at left, **$250-$300;** doll at right, **$150-$200.**

Washington Redskins, 1968-1970 NFL/AFL merger
series, two of four variations, **$200-$250.**

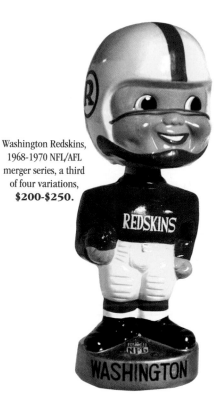

Washington Redskins,
1968-1970 NFL/AFL
merger series, a third
of four variations,
**$200-$250.**

## 1960s Canadian Football League

The dolls in these series are some of the prettiest ever produced. Because the teams are Canadian and not as recognizable as the NFL and AFL teams, these dolls unfortunately do not enjoy the same popularity. There are a number of size and style variations for each team. The bases can be wood or papier-mâché and are standard and mini sizes. There is also a series that has mascot heads peeking out of a football body. They are some of the most unique looking dolls you will find. Prices range from $125-$250 for near mint examples of the standard dolls and from $250-$500 for the mascot head dolls. There were nine teams represented. The teams issued were the British Columbia Lions, Calgary Stamps, Edmonton Eskimos, Hamilton Tiger Cats, Montreal Allouettes, Ottowa Rough Riders, Saskatchewan Rough Riders, Toronto Argos and the Winnipeg Blue Bombers. They are one of the most under-rated bobbing head dolls in the hobby.

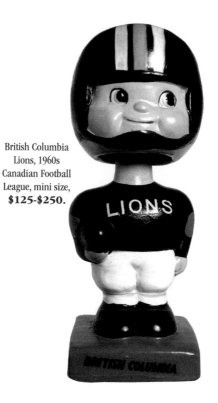

British Columbia
Lions, 1960s
Canadian Football
League, mini size,
**$125-$250.**

Calgary Stamps,
1960s Canadian
Football League,
**$125-$250.**

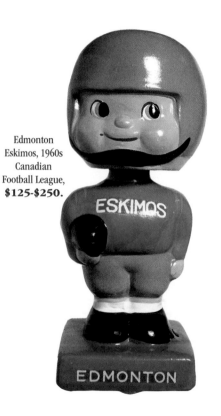

Edmonton
Eskimos, 1960s
Canadian
Football League,
**$125-$250.**

Hamilton Tiger Cats, 1960s Canadian Football
League, two variations, **$125-$250.**

Hamilton Tiger
Cats, 1960s
Canadian
Football League,
mascot head doll,
**$250-$500.**

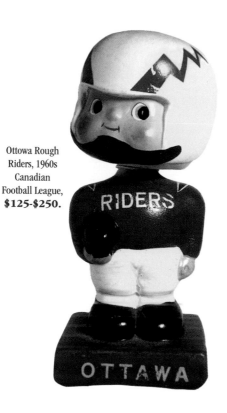

Ottowa Rough
Riders, 1960s
Canadian
Football League,
**$125-$250.**

Ottowa Rough Riders, 1960s Canadian Football League, mascot head doll, **$250-$500.**

Saskatchewan Rough Riders, 1960s Canadian Football League, mascot head doll, **$250-$500.**

Toronto Argos,
1960s Canadian
Football League,
**$125-$250.**

Winnipeg Blue Bombers, 1960s Canadian Football
League, two variations, **$125-$250.**

## 1960s college football dolls

No one can be absolutely sure how many colleges were represented with bobbing heads, but suffice it to say, there are a lot. There are also quite a number of variations and some of the larger universities (i.e. Notre Dame) can have several different styles. The value of the college doll is not solely based on rarity, but sometimes the fan base of the school's football team. Dolls from schools of the larger conferences (Big Ten, Pac 10, Ivy League etc.) usually attract more attention than the smaller schools and will command a higher price regardless of the rarity. Any price guide issued would be purely subjective and incomplete, but a good rule of thumb is, the bigger the school, the bigger the price. Prices of the college dolls usually range anywhere from $100 up to $500 for the harder to find variations. Within the college football series, there are some very special dolls that really excite advanced collectors. In particular are the nine known mascot head dolls (see list and prices below). They are absolutely spectacular and are one of the few football dolls that feature mascot heads and bodies.

| College mascots | EX/NM | College mascots | EX/NM |
| --- | --- | --- | --- |
| Arizona State Sun Devils | $350/$500 | North Texas State Eagles | $450/$600 |
| Baylor Bears (two styles) | $450/$600 | Pacific Tigers | $750/$1,000 |
| | | Stanford Indian | $750/$1,000 |
| California Bears | $450/$600 | Texas Longhorns | $500/$750 |
| LSU Tigers | $1,000/$1,500 | Washington State Cougars | $1,500/$2,000 |

Arizona State
Sun Devils, 1960s
college football
doll, mascot head,
**$350-$500.**

Baylor Bears, 1960s college football doll, mascot head (two styles), **$450-$600.**

California Bears,
1960s college
football doll,
mascot head,
**$450-$600.**

Columbia
University Lions,
1960s college
football doll,
**$100-$500.**

Cornell University,
1960s college
football doll,
**$100-$500.**

Dartmouth
College,
1960s college
football doll,
**$100-$500.**

Kansas State
University Wildcats,
1960s college
football doll,
**$100-$500.**

Navy, 1960s college
football doll,
**$100-$500.**

Stanford University Indian, 1960s college football doll, mascot head, **$750-$1,000.**

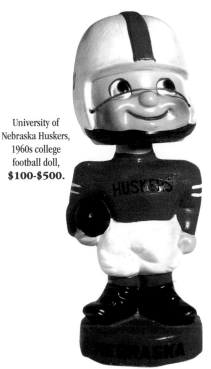

University of
Nebraska Huskers,
1960s college
football doll,
**$100-$500.**

University of
Washington Huskies,
1960s college football
doll, **$100-$500.**

## Newer issues of football bobbing heads

Just like the baseball dolls, there are a number of football dolls that were issued following the Golden Age of the 1960s. The 1970s brought a number of plastic dolls with several different head types and body styles. Advanced collectors tend to stay away from these dolls. These dolls can be bought in the $20-$40 range. Companies like SAM's and team-issued player dolls have become popular over the last 15 years, but prices are reasonable (under $50 each) because of the quantities made. Over the last decade or so, there have been issues of some college mascot dolls made of resin. Although they are terrific looking and feature mascots from each school, they are being made in large quantities and sell for about $25 each.

Miami Hurricanes mascot ibis head dolls, newer issues, **$25.**

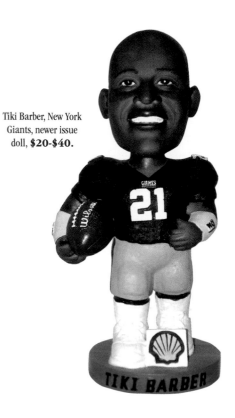

Tiki Barber, New York Giants, newer issue doll, **$20-$40.**

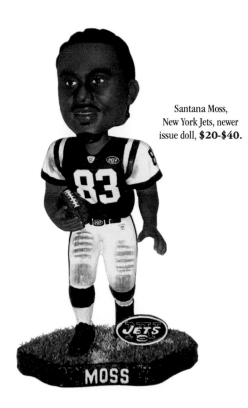

Santana Moss,
New York Jets, newer
issue doll, **$20-$40.**

# Hockey Bobbing Heads

Because of the richness of the colors of their uniforms, hockey bobbing heads are some of the most beautiful to collect. They are also popular among collectors because of the relatively small number of teams in the 1960s, and therefore not all that many dolls to obtain. Even when the NHL expanded in 1967 to 12 teams, the dolls were limited to only eight. Of more interest, though, is some of the minor league and European teams which can be quite difficult to find.

## 1961-1963 NHL square base

During this time period, the NHL consisted of only six teams. All of the teams are represented in both standard size and a miniature series. All are relatively common with the exceptions being the Boston Bruins standard size and the nearly impossible to find N.Y. Rangers mini. There was a small find of NHL minis with the exception of the Rangers. Be careful when buying this doll, as there are a number of fakes (always make sure that New York is painted on the base and not a decal).

| Team | Standard size | Miniature |
|------|---------------|-----------|
| Boston Bruins | $450/$600 | $80/$100 |
| Chicago Black Hawks | $250/$350 | $60/$85 |
| Detroit Red Wings | $250/$350 | $60/$85 |
| Montreal Canadiens | $125/$150 | $40/$60 |
| New York Rangers | $150/$200 | $1,000/$1,500 |
| Toronto Maple Leafs | $200/$250 | $60/$85 |

Boston Bruins, 1961-63 NHL square base, miniature, left,
**$80-$100;** and square base, standard size, **$450-$600.**

Chicago Black Hawks, 1961-63 NHL square base, miniature, left,
**$60-$85;** and square base, standard size, **$250-$350.**

Detroit Red Wings, 1961-63 NHL square base, miniature, left,
**$60-$85;** and square base, standard size, **$250-$350.**

Montreal Canadiens, 1961-63 NHL square base, miniature, left,
**$40-$60;** and square base, standard size, **$125-$150.**

New York Rangers, 1961-63 NHL square base, miniature. The authentic doll is on the right, **$1,000-$1,500.** The doll on the left is a fake.

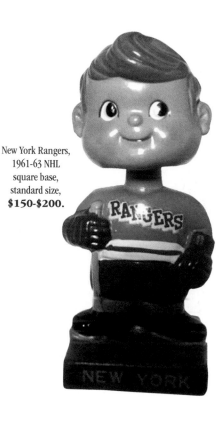

New York Rangers,
1961-63 NHL
square base,
standard size,
**$150-$200.**

Toronto Maple Leafs, 1961-63 NHL square base, miniature,
**$60-$85;** and square base, standard size, **$200-$250.**

## 1961-1963 NHL "High Skates" series

This series is very similar looking to the NHL Square base series and not easy for new collectors to distinguish. Again, there are only the "Original 6" NHL teams represented in two different sizes, a standard size and an intermediate size. There are three major differences between this series and the NHL square base. The first is the slightly different head style. This doll's ears protrude out much wider than the square base series. The second difference is in the title of the doll—its skates stand taller above the base. The third difference is on the base of the standard doll. Unlike the square base standard doll, the "high skate" doll has no city name on the base. This series is a lot harder to complete than the more common square base NHL dolls, with particular scarcity in the intermediate-sized dolls.

| Team | Standard | Intermediate |
|------|----------|--------------|
| Boston Bruins | $450/$600 | $450/$600 |
| Chicago Black Hawks | $350/$500 | $350/$500 |
| Detroit Red Wings | $350/$500 | $450/$600 |
| Montreal Canadiens | $200/$300 | $450/$600 |
| New York Rangers | $350/$500 | $450/$600 |
| Toronto Maple Leafs | $200/$300 | $350/$500 |

Boston Bruins, 1961-63 NHL "High Skates" series, standard
size, **$450-$600;** and intermediate size, **$450-$600.**

Chicago Black Hawks, 1961-63 NHL "High Skates" series, standard size, **$350-$500;** and intermediate size, **$350-$500.**

Detroit Red Wings, 1961-63 NHL "High Skates" series, standard size, **$350-$500;** and intermediate size, **$450-$600.**

Montreal Canadiens, 1961-63 NHL "High Skates" series, standard
size, **$200-$300;** and intermediate size, **$450-$600.**

New York Rangers, 1961-63 NHL "High Skates" series, standard
size, **$350-$500;** and intermediate size, **$450-$600.**

Toronto Maple Leafs, 1961-63 NHL "High Skates" series, standard
size, **$200-$300;** and intermediate size, **$350-$500.**

## 1967-1968 NHL realistic face

These dolls are just plain pretty. They all stand on a round gold base and feature a more mature realistic face. Many fans liken the faces to NHL stars Gordie Howe, Bobby Hull and Bobby Orr, but they are absolutely generic. The coloring is sharp and the chest decals are fabulous looking. Although the league had expanded to 12 teams, only eight are represented, with the St. Louis Blues having two uniform variations. For the most part, these dolls are not easy to find.

**1967-68 Gold base**

| Team | EX/NM |
|------|-------|
| Boston Bruins | $450/$600 |
| Chicago Blackhawks | $250/$350 |
| Detroit Redwings | $250/$350 |
| Los Angeles Kings | $350/$500 |
| Montreal Canadiens | $450/$600 |
| New York Rangers | $500/$750 |
| St. Louis Blues (gold) | $450/$600 |
| St. Louis Blues (blue) | $350/$500 |
| Toronto Maple Leafs | $500/$750 |

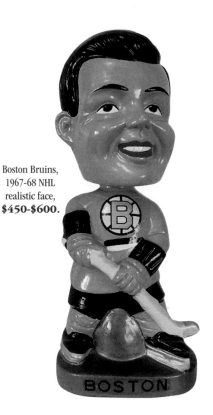

Boston Bruins,
1967-68 NHL
realistic face,
**$450-$600.**

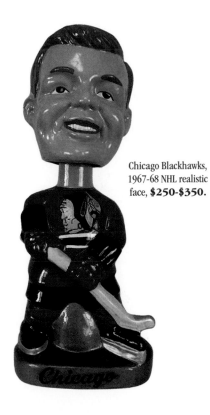

Chicago Blackhawks,
1967-68 NHL realistic
face, **$250-$350.**

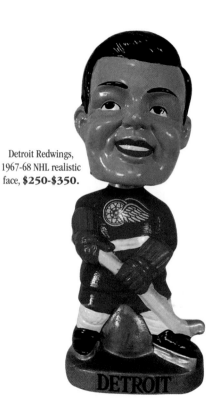

Detroit Redwings,
1967-68 NHL realistic
face, **$250-$350.**

Los Angeles Kings,
1967-68 NHL realistic
face, **$350-$500.**

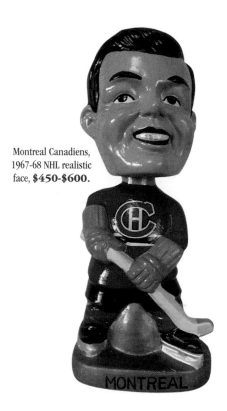

Montreal Canadiens,
1967-68 NHL realistic
face, **$450-$600.**

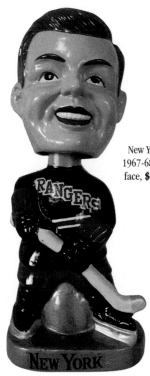

New York Rangers,
1967-68 NHL realistic
face, **$500-$750.**

St. Louis Blues, 1967-68 NHL realistic face, gold uniform,
**$450-$600;** blue uniform, **$350-$500.**

Toronto Maple Leafs, 1967-68 NHL realistic face, **$500-$750.**

## 1960s/early 1970s independent hockey dolls

There are a number of hockey dolls that really do not fit into any specific series. They can be of minor league teams, European teams, WHA or even some oddball NHL dolls. There are some that are so unusual in their looks that they far exceed the value of the traditional NHL dolls.

| Team | EX/NM | Team | EX/NM |
|---|---|---|---|
| AIK Rats (Swedish League) | $400/$500 | Los Angeles Blades | $250/$300 |
| Baltimore Clippers, mascot captain's head | $300/$350 | New England Whalers | $500/$750 |
| | | New York Rangers (jumbo sized, ceramic) | $250/$300 |
| Buffalo Braves | $450/$600 | New York Rangers (Blinker, only one known) | $1,500/$2,000 |
| Boston Bruins | $250/$300 | | |
| Boston Bruins (Blinker, only one known) | $1,500/$2000 | Port Huron Flags | $500/$750 |
| | | Portland Bucks | $500/$750 |
| Brynas Tigers (Swedish league) | $400/$500 | Salt Lake City Eagles | $1,500/$2,000 |
| Cleveland Crusaders (WHA) | $250/$300 | San Diego Gulls (mascot head, two color variations) | $400/$500 |
| Detroit Red Wings (Blinker, only one known) | $1,500/$2,000 | Toronto Maple Leafs (Blinker, only one known) | $1,500/$2,000 |
| FBK Wolves (Swedish League) | $400/$500 | Tre Kronor (Swedish league) | $400/$500 |
| Hershey Bears | $350/$450 | VIK Black Eagles (Swedish league) | $400/$500 |
| Johnstown Jets | $400/$500 | | |

Baltimore Clippers, mascot captain's head, 1960s/early 1970s independent hockey dolls, **$300-$350.**

Cleveland Crusaders
(WHA), 1960s/early
1970s independent
hockey dolls,
**$250-$300.**

Detroit Red Wings Blinker, only one known, 1960s/early 1970s independent hockey dolls, **$1,500-$2,000.**

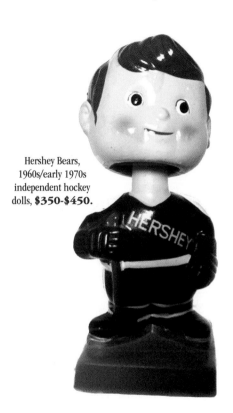

Hershey Bears,
1960s/early 1970s
independent hockey
dolls, **$350-$450.**

Johnstown Jets,
1960s/early 1970s
independent
hockey dolls,
**$400-$500.**

Los Angeles Blades,
1960s/early 1970s
independent
hockey dolls,
**$250-$300.**

New England
Whalers, 1960s/
early 1970s
independent
hockey dolls,
**$500-$750.**

Portland Bucks, 1960s/early 1970s independent hockey dolls, **$500-$750.**

Salt Lake City Eagles, 1960s/early 1970s independent hockey
dolls, front and side views, **$1,500-$2,000.**

San Diego Gulls, 1960s/early 1970s independent hockey dolls, mascot head, two color variations for pants, teal and red, **$400-$500.**

Swedish League, 1960s/early 1970s independent hockey dolls, AIK
Rats, left, **$400-$500;** and Brynas Tigers, **$400-$500.**

Swedish league, 1960s/early 1970s independent hockey dolls, Tre
Kronor, left, **$400-$500;** and VIK Black Eagles, **$400-$500.**

## Newer hockey dolls

There's not much to talk about here. There were no hockey dolls issued during the 1970s and until SAM's and teams started producing dolls in the 1990s, there was nothing in between. These dolls do not match the quality and good looks of the vintage dolls and their value is minimal. They usually retail in the $20-$40 range with few exceptions. Be careful, as there is an enterprising unlicensed maker who is making dolls and selling them with the hint that they may be vintage. They are a slightly heavier composition.

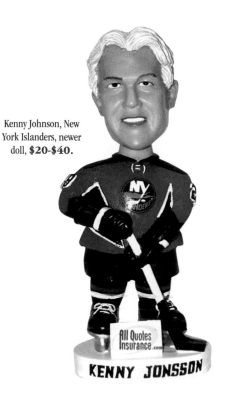

Kenny Johnson, New York Islanders, newer doll, **$20-$40.**

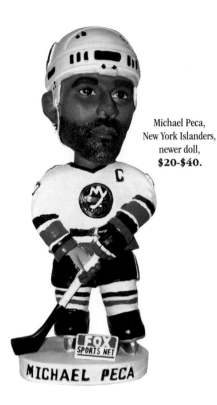

Michael Peca,
New York Islanders,
newer doll,
**$20-$40.**

# Other Bobbing Heads, Non-Team Sports

Team sports were not the only sports represented with bobbing heads. There are a host of other dolls made for activities like bowling, golf, car racing and even horse racing. Although not as popular as the team sports dolls, there are a few that draw a lot of attention. There are two dolls from the Indianapolis 500 that are exceptional. One features an Indy 500 driver in a car. This doll can sell for between $350 and $500. The other is just of an Indy 500 driver and it can also sell in the same range. Dolls that feature golfers have always been popular. There are a minimum of 25 different variations and they usually command a price tag of anywhere from $50 up to $200. There is a fabulous looking horse racing jockey that comes in several different colors that sells for about $75. There are many bowling dolls that are usually comical in nature. They will generally sell for $50 or less. To a lesser degree, there are generic dolls of tennis and fishing which do not have a big collectible value.

Non-team sport bobbing heads, bowling pair, each one **$50 or less.**

Non-team sport bobbing heads, bowling dolls, **$50 or less.**

These generic fishing non-team sport bobbing
heads do not have a big collectible value.

Dolls that feature golfers usually command a
price of between **$50 to $200.**

Non-team sport bobbing heads, Indy 500 driver in a car,
**$350-$500;** Indy 500 driver, **$350-$500.**

Non-team sport bobbing heads, two of several horse-racing jockeys that come in different colors, **$75.**

# Other Bobbing Heads, Non-Sports

There are so many different non-sport dolls, it would be impossible to catalog all or for that matter know exactly how many were made. The more popular dolls for collectors are ones that have specific themes. Advertising, political, television and movie stars and cartoon characters are some of the favorites of collectors. Because these themes have a crossover collectible appeal (bobbing heads with advertising, bobbing heads with political), their values can increase because of multiple interest groups. There are also a number of humorous dolls that have become popular over the years. Some of the less interesting bobbing dolls are virtually worthless, so be careful what you pay. The non-sports dolls can be really a blast to collect as you'll never quite be sure if you are finished. The following lists and pictures are by no means complete but will give you an idea of the kinds of dolls that are out there.

## Advertising

As mentioned, advertising dolls definitely are a crossover collectible appealing to bobbing head collectors and collectors of advertising memorabilia. Dolls of this genre can be of restaurants, retail companies, attractions or events. Some are quite unique looking, as they incorporate company mascots.

| Doll | EX/NM |
|------|-------|
| Ben Franklin bank (large size) | $50/$75 |
| Big Boy Restaurant | $450/$600 |
| Big Tex (from Texas State Fair, movable arm) | $150/$200 |
| Brylcreem (kissing pair) | $450/$600 |
| Democratic and Republican parties (donkey and elephant) | $75/$100 |
| Falls City Beer (large beer bottle that nods at waist) | $300/$400 |
| Groton Naval Base (Subby) | $300/$400 |
| Happy Homer | $350/$500 |
| Inky Dinky (Ice Follies) | $125/$150 |
| KC Piston | $300/$400 |
| Kentucky Fried Chicken (Colonel Sanders) | $150/$200 |
| Knott's Berry Farm | $300/$400 |
| L.A. County Fair (pig with suitcase) | $200/$250 |
| Little Profit (Chrysler) | $100/$125 |
| Mr. Peanut (with removable cane) | $200/$250 |
| NBC Wavy | $350/$500 |
| New York World's Fair, 1964-65 | |
|    Unisphere | $100/$125 |
|    Kissing pair | $200/$250 |
| Phillips 66 | $450/$600 |

| Doll | EX/NM |
|------|-------|
| Polly Parrot | $450/$600 |
| Reddy Kilowatt | $750/$1,000 |
| Red Goose Shoes (hip nodder) | $350/$500 |
| Rocky Taconite (heavy doll with taconite finish) | $350/$500 |
| Shriners (there are quite a number of different dolls) | $25/$50 |
| Six Flags | |
|    Miss Six Flags | $450/$600 |
|    Mexican with sombrero | $450/$600 |
| Smokey the Bear (several variations) | $200/$250 |
| Sparks, Nevada Nugget Casino | $250/$300 |
| Suzy Smart (there are least five dolls in this series) | $350/$500 |
| Tom Pouce Restaurant (Canadian eatery) | $500/$750 |
| Universal Studios | |
|    Director | $100/$125 |
|    Keystone Cop | $100/$125 |
| Phantom of Opera, different from the standard size | $400/$600 |
| Wally Waterlung (scuba gear) | $300/$400 |
| Weatherbird Shoes | $350/$500 |

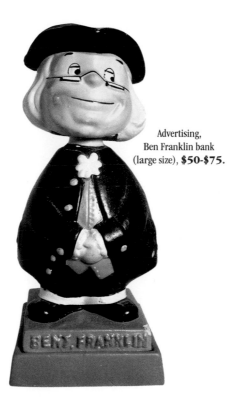

Advertising,
Ben Franklin bank
(large size), **$50-$75.**

Advertising,
Big Boy Restaurant,
**$450-$600.**

Advertising, Big Tex
with movable arm,
Texas State Fair,
**$150-$200.**

Advertising, Democratic and Republican parties
(donkey and elephant), **$75-$100 each.**

Advertising, Groton
Naval Base, Subby,
**$300-$400.**

Advertising,
Happy Homer,
**$350-$500.**

Advertising, Inky Dinky (Ice Follies), **$125-$150.**

Advertising,
KC Piston,
**$300-$400.**

Advertising, KFC,
Colonel Sanders,
**$150-$200.**

OUR COLONEL

Advertising, Knott's
Berry Farm,
**$300-$400.**

Advertising, Little
Profit, Chrysler,
**$100-$125.**

Advertising,
Mr. Peanut, with
removable cane,
**$200-$250.**

Advertising, NBC Wavy,
**$350-$500.**

Advertising, New York World's Fair, 1964-65 Unisphere, **$100-$125.**

Advertising, Universal Studios, Phantom of Opera, different from the standard size, **$400-$600.**

Advertising,
Phillips 66,
**$450-$600.**

Advertising, Red
Goose Shoes
(hip nodder),
**$350-$500.**

Advertising, Rocky Taconite, heavy doll with taconite finish, **$350-$500.**

Advertising, Shriners, three of many different dolls, **$25-$50.**

Advertising, Shriners, three more of many
different variations, **$25-$50.**

Advertising, Six
Flags, Miss Six Flags,
**$450-$600.**

Advertising, Smokey
the Bear (several
variations),
**$200-$250.**

Advertising,
Sparks, Nevada
Nugget Casino,
**$250-$300.**

Advertising, Suzy Smart, two of at least five
dolls in this series, **$350-$500.**

Advertising, Suzy Smart, three of at least five
dolls in this series, **$350-$500.**

Advertising, Tom
Pouce Restaurant
(Canadian eatery),
**$500-$750.**

Advertising, Universal
Studios, Director,
**$100-$125.**

Advertising, Universal
Studios, Keystone
Cop, **$100-$125.**

Advertising,
Wally Waterlung
(scuba gear),
**$300-$400.**

Advertising,
Weatherbird Shoes,
**$350-$500.**

# Cartoon and comic strip characters

These dolls are fun for almost everybody as they feature the characters that were so popular during our youth. There are several series including Disney, Peanuts, Beetle Bailey and Warner Brothers. Completing the sets increases the values of the individual dolls.

| Doll | EX/NM |
|---|---|
| Batman (only two known) | $5,000/$7,500 |
| Beetle Bailey (Beetle Bailey, Sgt Snorkel, Lt Fuzz and Zero) | $600 set of four dolls |
| Bozo the Clown | $1,250/$1,500 |
| Dick Tracy | $3,500/$5,000 |
| **Disney characters** | |
| Donald Duck | |
| Square green base | $350/$500 |
| Round green base | $75/$100 |
| White base-Disneyland | $200/$250 |
| White base-Walt Disney World | $150/4200 |
| Goofy | |
| Disneyland | $150/$200 |
| Walt Disney World | $125/$150 |
| Mickey Mouse | |
| Square green base | $350/$500 |
| Disneyland | $150/$200 |
| Walt Disney World | $100/$125 |
| On motorcycle with duck, ceramic | $250/$300 |
| Pluto | $75/$100 |
| Winnie the Pooh | $150/$200 |
| 101 Dalmatians | $125/$150 |
| Lil Abner (Mammy and Pappy Yokum, ceramic) | $75/$100 |
| Mr. Magoo | $3,500/$5,000 |
| Oodles the Duck (from the Bozo cartoon) | $750/$1,000 |

| Doll | EX/NM |
|---|---|
| **Peanuts characters** | |
| Charlie Brown | |
| Black base | $125/$150 |
| Mini size, no base | $50/$75 |
| Linus (black base) | $125/$150 |
| Lucy | |
| Black base | $125/$150 |
| Mini size, no base | $50/$75 |
| Pig Pen (black base) | $200/$300 |
| Schroeder (black base) | $200/$300 |
| Snoopy | |
| Black base | $100/$125 |
| Three different mini size, no base, Santa, Joe Cool and Red Baron | $35/$50 |
| Woodstock (mini size, no base) | $35/$50 |
| **Warner Brothers characters** | |
| Bugs Bunny | $300/$400 |
| Daffy Duck | $750/$1,000 |
| Elmer Fudd | $400/$500 |
| Foghorn Leghorn | $300/$400 |
| Popeye | $3,500/$5,000 |
| Porky Pig | $250/$300 |
| Robin (from Batman) | $3,500/$5,000 |
| Speedy Gonzales | $500/$750 |
| Tweety | $400/$500 |
| Wile E Coyote | $300/$400 |
| Yosemite Sam | $400/$500 |

Cartoon and comic strip characters, Beetle Bailey, Lt. Fuzz, Zero and
Sgt. Snorkel, **$600 set of four dolls.** Missing is Beetle Bailey.

Cartoon and comic strip characters, Dick Tracy, **$3,500-$5,000.**

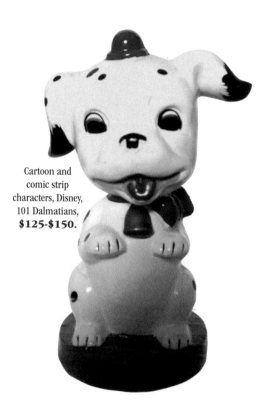

Cartoon and
comic strip
characters, Disney,
101 Dalmatians,
**$125-$150.**

Cartoon and comic strip characters, Disney, Donald Duck, square green base, **$350-$500;** and white Walt Disney World base, **$150-$200.**

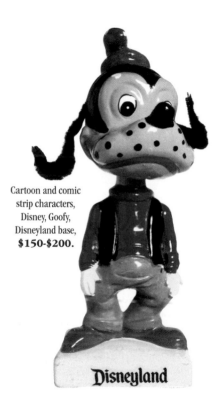

Cartoon and comic
strip characters,
Disney, Goofy,
Disneyland base,
**$150-$200.**

Cartoon and comic strip characters, Disney, Mickey Mouse, green base, **$350-$500;** and Walt Disney World base, **$100-$125.**

Cartoon and comic strip characters, Disney, Mickey Mouse,
on motorcycle with duck, ceramic, **$250-$300.**

Cartoon and comic strip characters, Disney, Pluto, **$75-$100.**

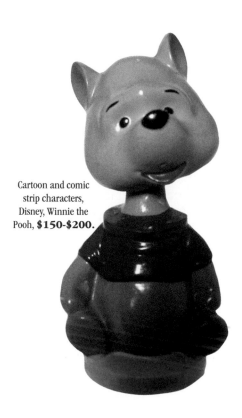

Cartoon and comic strip characters, Disney, Winnie the Pooh, **$150-$200.**

Cartoon and comic strip characters, Peanuts, Charlie Brown, black base, **$125-$150;** and mini size, no base, **$50-$75.**

Cartoon and comic strip characters, Peanuts, Linus, black base, **$125-$150.**

Cartoon and comic strip characters, Peanuts, Lucy, black base,
**$125-$150;** and mini size, no base, **$50-$75.**

Cartoon and comic strip characters, Peanuts, Pig Pen, black base, **$200-$300.**

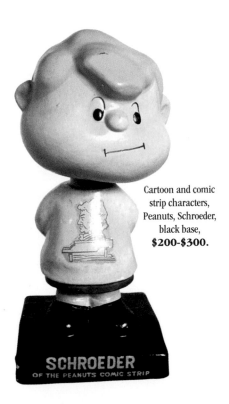

Cartoon and comic strip characters, Peanuts, Schroeder, black base, **$200-$300.**

Cartoon and comic strip characters, Peanuts, Snoopy,
two of three different mini size dolls, no base, Red Baron
and Santa, **$35-$50.** The third doll is Joe Cool.

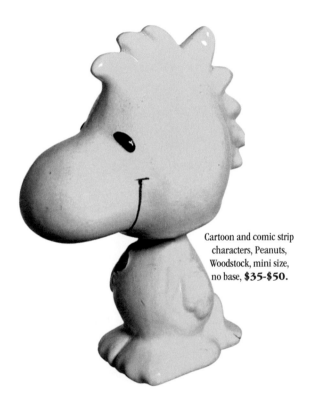

Cartoon and comic strip
characters, Peanuts,
Woodstock, mini size,
no base, **$35-$50.**

Cartoon and comic
strip characters,
Warner Brothers,
Bugs Bunny,
**$300-$400.**

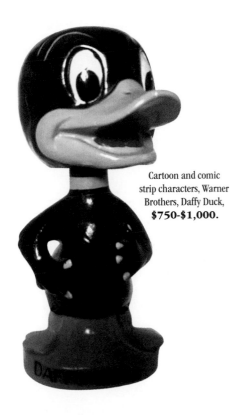

Cartoon and comic
strip characters, Warner
Brothers, Daffy Duck,
**$750-$1,000.**

Cartoon and comic
strip characters,
Warner Brothers,
Elmer Fudd,
**$400-$500.**

Cartoon and comic strip characters, Warner Brothers, Foghorn Leghorn, **$300-$400.**

Cartoon and comic strip characters, Warner Brothers, Porky Pig, **$250-$300.**

Cartoon and comic
strip characters,
Warner Brothers,
Speedy Gonzales,
**$500-$750.**

Cartoon and comic
strip characters,
Warner Brothers,
Tweety, **$400-$500.**

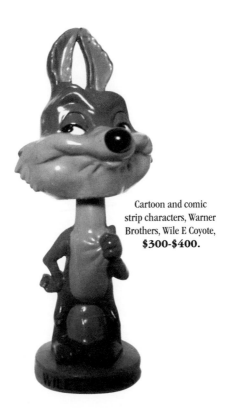

Cartoon and comic strip characters, Warner Brothers, Wile E Coyote, **$300-$400.**

Cartoon and
comic strip
characters,
Warner Brothers,
Yosemite Sam,
**$400-$500.**

## Personalities—movies/TV, music and political

During the early 1960s, the Cold War was in full bloom and almost every American home had at least one television set and political figures and television personalities became recognizable. The makers of bobbing head dolls cashed in on this fame by producing a number of dolls with themes ranging from TV and movie stars to the political genre. These are some of the most sought after dolls and again have the crossover potential many collectors love.

| Movies/TV and musical personalities | EX/NM |
|---|---|
| Beatles (set of four, add $250 w/box) | $600/$750 |
| Ben Casey | $75/$100 |
| Cantinflas (Mexican actor from the movie "Pepe") | $300/$400 |
| Charlie Weaver | $150/$200 |
| Danny Kaye (kissing pair) | $350/$500 |
| Davy Crockett (probably a 1950s issue) | $250/$300 |
| Dobie Gillis | $300/$400 |
| Donnie Osmond (1970s large ceramic doll) | $150/$200 |
| Dr. Kildare | $75/$100 |
| Frankenstein | $2,500/$4,000 |
| Lad A Dog | $300/$400 |
| Maynard G. Krebs | $300/$400 |
| Phantom of the Opera | $2,000/$3,000 |
| Roy Rogers | $150/$200 |
| Wolfman | $2,500/$4,000 |

| Political figures | EX/NM |
|---|---|
| Castro, Fidel (in toilet) | $300/$400 |
| Castro, Fidel/ Khrushchev, Nikita (kissing pair) | $300/$400 |
| Eisenhower, Dwight D. | $250/$300 |
| Kennedy, JFK (playing football) | $750/$1,000 |
| Kennedys (Jack and Jackie, kissing pair) | $1,000/$1,250 |
| Khrushchev, Nikita | |
|    Banging shoe at podium | $450/$600 |
|    Castro's beard | $450/$600 |
| Mao | $750/$1,000 |
| Rockefeller (only two known) | $1,000/$1,500 |

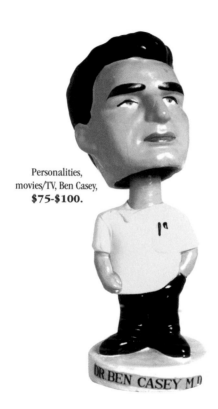

Personalities,
movies/TV, Ben Casey,
**$75-$100.**

Personalities, movies/TV, Charlie Weaver, **$150-$200.**

Personalities,
movies/TV, Dobie
Gillis, **$300-$400.**

Personalities, movies/TV, Dr. Kildare, **$75-$100.**

Personalities,
movies/TV, Frankenstein,
**$2,500-$4,000.**

Personalities,
movies/TV,
Lad A Dog,
**$300-$400.**

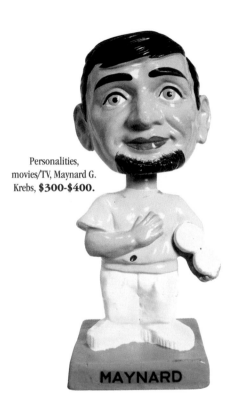

Personalities, movies/TV, Maynard G. Krebs, **$300-$400.**

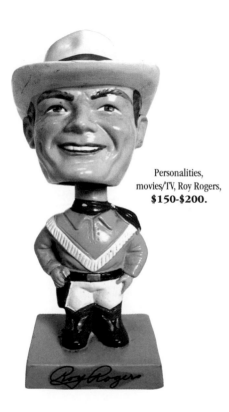

Personalities,
movies/TV, Roy Rogers,
**$150-$200.**

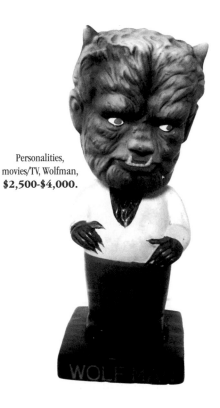

Personalities,
movies/TV, Wolfman,
**$2,500-$4,000.**

Personalities, music, Beatles, set of four, George Harrison and John Lennon pictured, **$600-$750 (add $250 with box).**

Personalities, music, Beatles, set of four, Paul McCartney and Ringo
Starr pictured, **$600-$750 (add $250 with box).**

Personalities, political, Fidel Castro, in toilet, **$300-$400.**

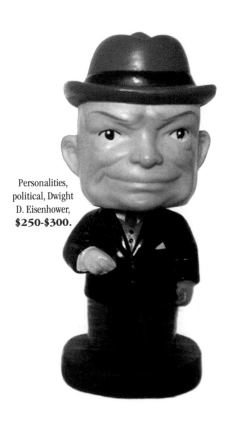

Personalities,
political, Dwight
D. Eisenhower,
**$250-$300.**

Personalities, political, Jackie and John F. Kennedy,
kissing pair, **$1,000-$1,250.**

Personalities, political,
John F. Kennedy,
playing football,
**$750-$1,000.**

Personalities, political, Nikita Khrushchev
and Fidel Castro, kissing pair, **$300-$400.**

Personalities, political, Nikita Khrushchev, Castro's beard, left,
**$450-$600;** banging shoe at podium, **$450-$600.**

## Novelty and humorous bobbing heads

There are literally hundreds of generic novelty dolls that were produced during the Golden Age with various themes. They range from ethnic kissing dolls to hilarious bums to the oddball ogres of the Rumpus Room series. There are more and more of these dolls surfacing every day. There's plenty to collect, but the good news is that they are relatively inexpensive compared to the sports and personality dolls. Most of these generic dolls are in the $25-$100 range, with only a few rare exceptions.

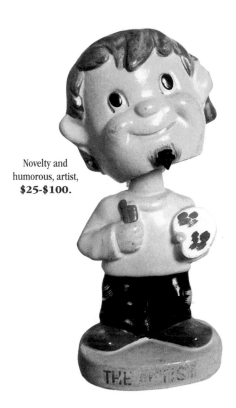

Novelty and
humorous, artist,
**$25-$100.**

THE ARTIST

Novelty and humorous, astronauts, two variations, **$25-$100.**

Novelty and humorous, two of several variations of bums, **$25-$100.**

Novelty and humorous, two more of several
bum variations, **$25-$100.**

Novelty and humorous, ethnic kissing dolls, Spain, **$25-$100.**

Novelty and
humorous, hillbilly,
**$25-$100.**

Novelty and
humorous,
medicine man,
**$25-$100.**

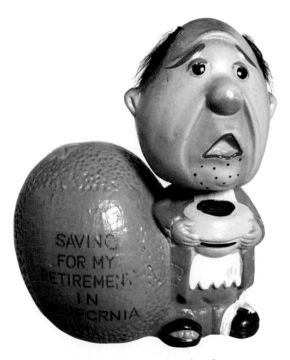

Novelty and humorous, retirement, **$25-$100.**

Novelty and humorous, elf, **$25-$100;** and
Frosty the Snowman, **$25-$100.**

Novelty and humorous, Santa in sled, **$25-$100.**

Novelty and
humorous, kissing
sailor, **$25-$100.**

Novelty and humorous, Rumpus Room series, bear,
**$25-$100;** and bowler, **$25-$100.**

Novelty and humorous, Rumpus Room series, boxer,
**$25-$100**; and clown, **$25-$100**.

Novelty and humorous, Rumpus Room series, doctor,
**$25-$100;** and golfer, **$25-$100.**

Novelty and humorous, Rumpus Room series, hag,
**$25-$100;** and knight, **$25-$100.**

Novelty and humorous, Rumpus Room series, "Mr. Sunshine" orange, **$25-$100;** and man under pressure, **$25-$100.**

Novelty and humorous, Rumpus Room series, man
frowning, **$25-$100;** and puppy, **$25-$100.**

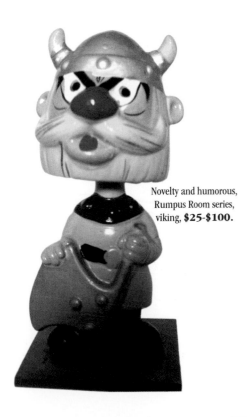

Novelty and humorous,
Rumpus Room series,
viking, **$25-$100.**

## The newer issues of non-sports bobbing heads

Like the other sports dolls, there have been plenty of newer non-sports resin dolls being produced over the last 10 years. There are movie, television and rock stars, as well as political personalities and company mascots. They're fun, but unless you stick to a theme, your collection may seem endless. The prices are still quite reasonable because of the large quantities being made; most can still be found for their original retail price, usually ranging between $10-$25, while some cost higher.

Newer issue doll,
Michelin Man,
retail price.

Newer issue dolls, Mikey and Paul Jr. from
Orange County Choppers, retail price.

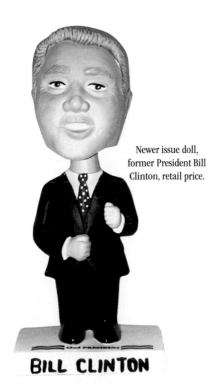

Newer issue doll,
former President Bill
Clinton, retail price.

**BILL CLINTON**

Newer issue doll, surfer, retail price.

Newer issue dolls, Three Stooges, Curly, Larry and Moe, retail price.

Newer issue
doll, Uncle Sam,
retail price.

DON'T MESS WITH THE U.S.